PATHWAYS TO PARKER

The Improvisational Patterns of Charlie Parker
(Treble Clef)

by

Dr. W. Terry Rowlyk

©

Copyright

2022

by

Dr. W. Terry Rowlyk Publications

All Rights Reserved

PATHWAYS TO PARKER

How to use this book and app:

This book and app were created to catalog the melodic pattern material performed by Charlie Parker for over sixty of his transcribed solos. The app, *Pathways to Parker*, mirrors the book. The teacher may use the text while the student can either use the text or the app at the same time.

The patterns are organized by the key and chord type in which they were originally performed. The performer may use the patterns at their discretion, in the original key, or transpose them as needed.

The teacher may use these patterns in a number of creative ways:

1. Instrumental sight-reading material.
2. Composition ideas
3. Examples of what musical ideas will work over an existing chord change.
4. Starting point for students to creatively connect the patterns in order to expand their music vocabulary.
5. Starting point for the development of written solos within the developing jazz band.
6. Analysis of the most widely-used key and chord centers in Charlie Parker's repertoire.
7. Abstraction and insertion of Charlie Parker's vocabulary into existing solos to create new ones.
8. Provision of new source material for the professional musician who would like to expand their jazz vocabulary.

© 2022 Dr. W. Terry Rowlyk Publications. All Rights Reserved.

All patterns are one measure in length. Patterns may be joined together as the improviser sees fit, however, proper voice leading and chaining of patterns will produce more musical ideas.

Rationale:

As a music educator with 30 years of experience, I have witnessed and worked with students who have a desire to learn jazz improvisation, but have a very limited jazz vocabulary. With proper guidance, *Pathways to Parker* may become an essential new resource by which students can learn, internalize, and apply musical ideas in unique ways.

Thank you:

- To my wife Kimberly (Holody) Rowlyk and to my sons Alden and Wyatt;
- To my parents Wasyl and Carol Rowlyk;
- To my siblings David and Tara and their spouses and children;
- To Denis DiBlasio for his inspiration through his improvisation text "Pathways to Improvisation."
- To the Ridley School District Administration and Music Department
- To Deborah Confredo for her advice;
- To *"West Chester Music Service Learning Center"* staff Marci Major and student contributor Devon Rickert.

Review of Related Literature

      This book was developed by the author through extensive research in the area of musical improvisation and achievement among instrumental music students. Academic commentary supports the theory that the learning and practicing of improvisational techniques enables students to develop ideas for the creation of their own improvisations and musical compositions. The study of pre-inventive musical patterns, consisting of chordal, tonal, and rhythmic elements, allow students to reach maximum musical ability. Indeed, cognitive scientists have remarked that the learning processes that define "creativity" involve generating, refining, combining, and transforming familiar elements in unique ways.

      Designed to facilitate the creative musical process, the author of *Pathways to Parker* organizes, categorizes, and transforms the improvisational material of Charlie Parker in a way that will help guide students and performers to make educated decisions while improvising, composing, or performing musical compositions. The chordal, tonal, and rhythmic patterns that are featured in Charlie Parker's music serve as a starting point for students who are looking to expand and build upon their own music vocabulary.

Table of Contents

PATHWAYS TO PARKER — 1
How to use this book and app: — 1
Rationale: — 2
Thank you: — 2
Review of Related Literature — 3
Table of Contents — 4
Contents by Alphabetical Order Summary Chart: — 10
Contents by Alphabetical Order: — 11
Contents by Alphabetical Order Continued: — 12
Contents by Alphabetical Order Continued: — 13
Chapter #1 — 15
Major Chords and Progressions — 15
Major Chords: — 15
Ab Major — 15
A Major — 17
Bb Major — 28
C Major — 35
D Major — 50
E Major — 78
F Major — 82
F# Major (Gb Major) — 91
G Major — 93

Major Progressions: — 150

Major to Major: — 150
C to Ab — 150

Major to Dominant 7: — 150
C to A7 — 150
C to C7 — 151
D to B7 — 152
D to G7 — 153
F to D7 — 154
F to F7 — 155
G to E7 — 156

Major to Dominant 7b9: — 162
- A to F#7b9 — 162
- G to E7b9 — 162

Major to Minor: — 163
- Bb to Bb min — 163
- C to C min — 164
- G to Bb min — 165

Major to Minor to Dominant 7: — 166
- C to B min to E7 — 166

Major to Fully Diminished: — 166
- A to C 0 (Fully Diminished) — 166
- C to C# 07 (Fully Diminished) — 167

Chapter #2 — 168
Dominant 7 Chords and Progressions — 168

Dominant 7 Chords: — 168
- Ab7 — 168
- A7 — 169
- Bb7 — 227
- B7 — 231
- C7 — 249
- C#7 (Db7) — 276
- D7 — 279
- Eb7 — 340
- E7 — 342
- F7 — 369
- F#7 (Gb7) — 386
- G7 — 392

Dominant 7b9 Chords: — 459
- A7b9 — 459
- D7b9 — 460
- E7 b9 — 464
- F#7b9 — 464

Dominant 7+9 Chords: — 465
- Ab7+9 — 465
- B7+9 — 465
- E7+9 — 466

Dominant 7b9+9 Chords: — 467

  D7b9+9 --- 467

Dominant 7 #11: --- **467**
  G7 #11 --- 467

Dominant 7 Progressions: --- **468**

Dominant 7 to Major: --- **468**
  C7 to Ab --- 468

Dominant 7 to Dominant 7: --- **469**
  A7 to E7 --- 469
  A7 to F#7 --- 469
  A7 to G7 --- 470
  C7 to A7 --- 471
  C7 to Bb7 --- 472
  C7 to C#7 --- 473
  C7 to G7 --- 473
  Db7 to D7 --- 473
  D7 to A7 --- 474
  D7 to B7 --- 474
  D7 to G7 --- 475
  Eb7 to E7 --- 475
  E7 to A7 --- 475
  G7 to D7 --- 476
  G7 to E7 --- 476

Dominant 7 to Dominant 7b9: --- **477**
  A7 to F#7b9 --- 477
  E7 to E7b9 --- 478
  G7 to E7b9 --- 478

Dominant 7 to Minor: --- **479**
  C7 to C min --- 479
  D7 to D min --- 480
  G7 to A min --- 480
  G7 to Bb min --- 481

Dominant 7 to Half Diminished 7: --- **481**
  C7 to C#ø7 --- 481

Dominant 7 to Fully Diminished: --- **482**
  C7 to C# 0 --- 482
  D7 to F#0 (Gb0) --- 483
  G7 to G0 --- 484
  G7 to G#0 (Ab0) --- 484

Dominant 7 to Augmented 7: 486
    C7 to C+7 486

Dominant 7 to Major to Fully Diminished: 487
    G7 to C to C#0 487

Dominant 7 to Dominant 7 to Fully Diminished: 487
    G7 to C7 to C#0 487

Dominant 7 to Minor to Dominant 7: 488
    G7 to Bb min to Eb7 488
    G7 to D min to G7 488

Dominant 7 Slash Chords: 489
    G7/D to D7 489

Chapter #3 490
Minor Chords and Progressions 490

Minor Chords: 490
    Ab minor 490
    A minor 491
    Bb minor 515
    B minor 517
    C minor 527
    C# minor 536
    D minor 538
    E minor 549
    F minor 573
    F# minor 575
    G minor 578
    G# minor 594

Minor Progressions: 595

Minor to Major: 595
    A min to Ab 595
    E min to Eb 595

Minor to Dominant 7: 596
    A min to D7 596
    A min to E7 642
    B min to B7 642
    B min to E7 643
    B min to F#7 665
    C min to B7 665

    C min to F7 -- 666
    C# min to F#7 -- 668
    D min to Db7 -- 673
    D min to G7 --- 673
    E min to A7 --- 689
    F min to Bb7 -- 709
    F# min to B7 -- 710
    G min to C7 --- 718
    G# min to C#7 -- 723

Minor to Dominant 7b9: -- **724**
    A min to D7b9 -- 724
    B min to E7b9 --- 724
    C# min to F#7b9 -- 724
    F# min to B7b9 --- 725

Minor to Dominant 7+9: --- **726**
    A min to D7+9 -- 726
    B min to F#7+9 --- 726
    E min to B7+9 --- 726

Minor to Minor: --- **727**
    A min to Ab min -- 727
    B min to Bb min -- 727
    D min to Db min -- 728
    F# min to F min -- 728

Minor to Augmented 7: --- **729**
    A min to D7#5 -- 729
    D min to G7#5 -- 730
    E min to A7#5 --- 730

Minor to Dominant 7 to Dominant 7+9: ----------------------------------- **731**
    E min to A7 to A7+9 -- 731

Chapter #4 -- *732*

Half Diminished 7 ⌀ (Minor 7 b5) Chords and Progressions: ------------------------- *732*

Half Diminished 7 ⌀ Chords: -- *732*
    E⌀7 --- 732

Half Diminished 7 ⌀ Progressions: --- *733*

Half Diminished 7 to Dominant 7: --- **733**
    A⌀7 to D7 --- 733
    B⌀7 to E7 -- 733

  C#ø7 to F#7 — 735
  D#ø7 to G#7 — 738
  E ø7 to A7 — 739
  F#ø7 to B7 — 739

 Half Diminished 7 to Dominant 7b9: — **740**
  B ø7 to E7b9 — 740

Half Diminished 7 to Dominant 7+9: — **741**
  D#ø to G#7+9 — 741

Chapter #5 — 742

Fully Diminished Chords — 742

 Fully Diminished Chords: — 742
  C 0 (Fully Diminished) — 742
  D 0 (Fully Diminished) — 743
  G# 0 (Fully Diminished) — 744

Chapter #6 — 745

Augmented Chords — 745

 Augmented Chords: — 745
  D+ — 745

 Augmented 7: — 745
  A+7 — 745
  C+7 — 746
  D+7 — 746
  G+7 — 747

 REFERENCES — 748

Contents by Alphabetical Order Summary Chart:

Ab Major	B7+9	C minor to B7	D+7	F# minor
Ab7	B minor	C minor to F7	D#ϕ to G#7	F# minor to B7
Ab7+9	B minor to Bb minor	C 0 (Fully Diminished)	D#ϕ to G#7+9	F# minor to B7b9
Ab minor	B minor to B7	C+7	Eb7	F# minor to F minor
A Major	B minor to E7	C#7 (Db7)	Eb7 to E7	F#ϕ to B7
A to F#7b9	B minor to E7b9	C# minor	E Major	G Major
A to C 0 (Fully Diminished)	B minor to F#7	C# minor to F#7	E7	G to E7
A7	B minor to F#7+9	C# minor to F#7b9	E7 to A7	G to E7b9
A7b9	Bϕ to E7	C#ϕ7 to F#7	E7 to E7b9	G to Bb minor
A7 to E 7	Bϕ to E7b9	Db7 to D7	E7b9	G7
A7 to F#7	C Major	D Major	E7+9	G7 to C to C# 0 (Fully Diminished)
A7 to F#7b9	C to Ab	D to B7	E minor	G7 to C7 to C# 0 (Fully Diminished)
A7 to G7	C to A7	D to G7	E minor to Eb	G7 to D7
A minor	C to C7	D7	E minor to A7	G7 to E7
A minor to Ab	C to B minor to E7	D7b9	E minor to A7 to A7+9	G7 to E7b9
A minor to Ab minor	C to C minor	D7 to A7	E minor to B7+9	G7 to G0 (Fully Diminished)
A minor to D7+	C to C# 0 7 (Fully Diminished 7)	D7 to B7	E minor to A+7	G7 to G#0 (Ab0)(Fully Diminished)
A minor to D7	C7	D7 to G7	Eϕ7	G7 to A minor
A minor to D7+9	C7 to Ab	D7 to D minor	Eϕ7 to A7	G7 to Bb minor
A minor to D7b9	C7 to A7	D7 to F# 0 (Gb 0) (Fully Diminished)	F Major	G7 to Bb minor to Eb7
A minor to E7	C7 to Bb7	D7b9+9	F to D7	G7 to D minor to G7
A ϕ7 to D7	C7 to C#7	D minor	F to F7	G7/D to D7
A7+	C7 to G7	D minor to Db 7	F7	G minor
Bb Major	C7 to C minor	D minor to G7	F minor	G minor to C7
Bb to Bb minor	C7 to C#ϕ7	D minor to Db minor	F minor to Bb7	G7+
Bb7	C7 to C# 0 7 (Fully Diminished 7)	D minor to G7+	F# Major (Gb Major)	G# minor
Bb minor	C7 to C7+	D 0 (Fully Diminished)	F#7 (Gb7)	G# minor to C#7
B7	C minor	D+	F#7b9	G# 0 (Fully Diminished)

Contents by Alphabetical Order:

Ab Major	15
Ab7	168
Ab7+9	465
Ab minor	490
A Major	17
A to F#7b9	162
A to C 0 (Fully Diminished)	166
A7	169
A7b9	459
A7 to E7	469
A7 to F#7	469
A7 to F#7b9	477
A7 to G7	470
A minor	491
A min to Ab	595
A min to Ab min	727
A min to D7#5	729
A min to D7	596
A min to D7+9	726
A min to D7b9	724
A min to E7	642
AØ7 to D7	733
A+7	745
Bb Major	28
Bb to Bb min	163
Bb7	227
Bb minor	515
B7	231
B7+9	465
B minor	517
B min to Bb min	727
B min to B7	642
B min to E7	643
B min to E7b9	724
B min to F#7	665
B min to F#7+9	726
BØ7 to E7	733
BØ7 to E7b9	740
C Major	35

Contents by Alphabetical Order Continued:

C to Ab	150
C to A7	150
C to C7	151
C to B min to E7	166
C to C min	164
C to C# 07 (Fully Diminished)	167
C7	249
C7 to Ab	468
C7 to A7	471
C7 to Bb7	472
C7 to C#7	473
C7 to G7	473
C7 to C min	479
C7 to C#ø7	481
C7 to C# 0	482
C7 to C+7	486
C minor	527
C min to B7	665
C min to F7	666
C 0 (Fully Diminished)	742
C+7	746
C#7 (Db7)	276
C# minor	536
C# min to F#7	668
C# min to F#7b9	724
C#ø7 to F#7	735
Db7 to D7	473
D Major	50
D to B7	152
D to G7	152
D7	279
D7b9	460
D7 to A7	474
D7 to B7	474
D7 to G7	475
D7 to D min	480
D7 to F#0 (Gb0)	483
D7b9+9	467
D minor	538

Contents by Alphabetical Order Continued:

D min to Db7	673
D min to G7	673
D min to Db min	728
D min to G7#5	730
D 0 (Fully Diminished)	743
D+	745
D+7	746
D#ø7 to G#7	738
D#ø to G#7+9	741
Eb7	340
Eb7 to E7	475
E Major	78
E7	342
E7 to A7	475
E7 to E7b9	478
E7 b9	464
E7+9	466
E minor	549
E min to Eb	595
E min to A7	689
E min to A7 to A7+9	731
E min to B7+9	726
E min to A7#5	730
E ø7	732
E ø7 to A7	739
F Major	82
F to D7	154
F to F7	155
F7	369
F minor	573
F min to Bb7	709
F# Major (Gb Major)	91
F#7 (Gb7)	386
F#7b9	464
F# minor	575
F# min to B7	710
F# min to B7b9	725
F# min to F min	728
F#ø7 to B7	739

G Major	93
G to E7	156
G to E7b9	162
G to Bb min	165
G7	392
G7 to C to C#0	487
G7 to C7 to C#0	487
G7 to D7	476
G7 to E7	476
G7 to E7b9	478
G7 to G0	484
G7 to G#0 (Ab0)	484
G7 to A min	480
G7 to Bb min	481
G7 to Bb min to Eb7	488
G7 to D min to G7	488
G7/D to D7	489
G7 #11	467
G minor	578
G min to C7	718
G+7	747
G# minor	594
G# min to C#7	723
G# 0 (Fully Diminished)	744

Chapter #1

Major Chords and Progressions

Major Chords:

Ab Major

9.

10.

A Major

1.

2.

25.

26.

27.

28.

29.

30.

Bb Major

5.

6.

7.

8.

9.

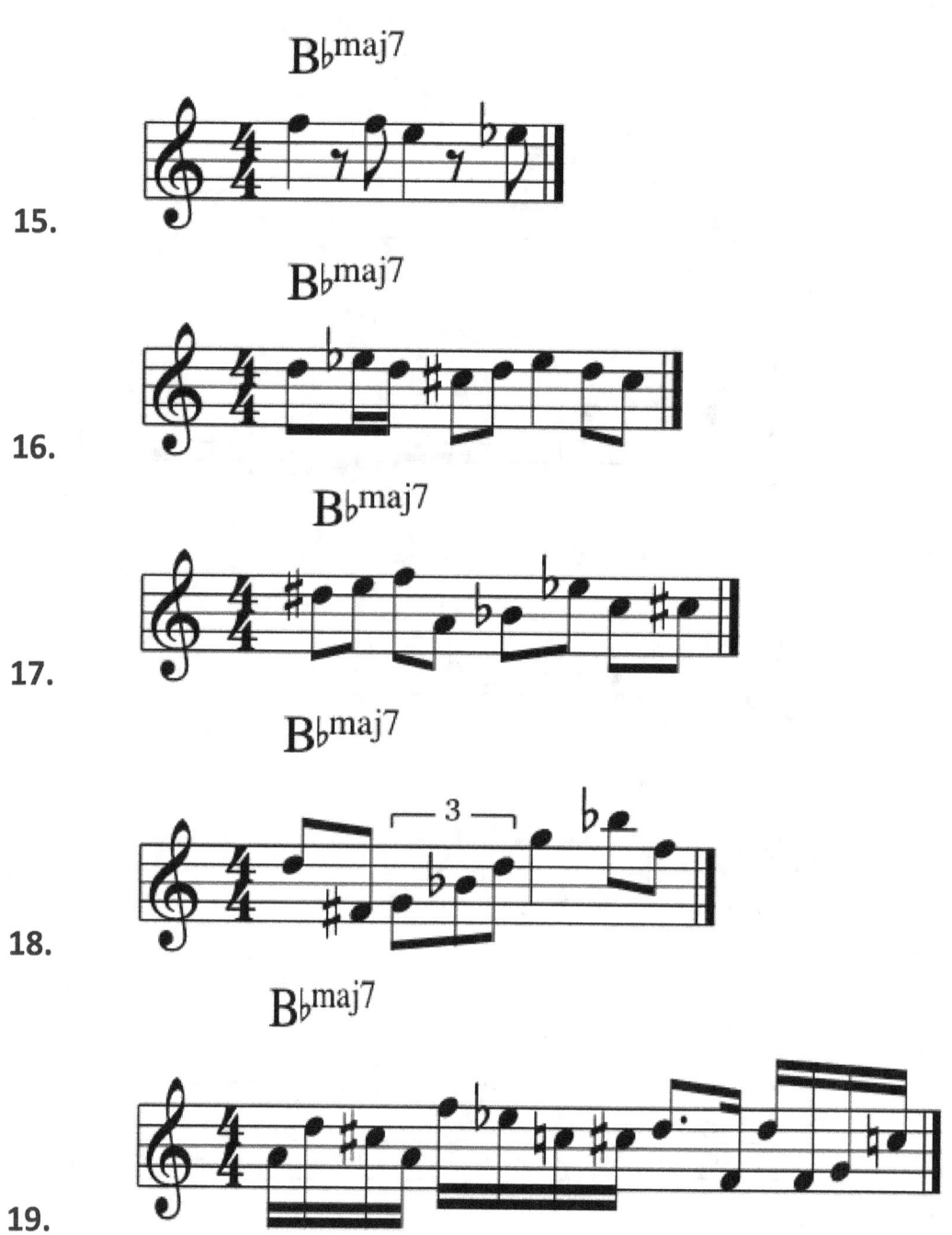

C Major

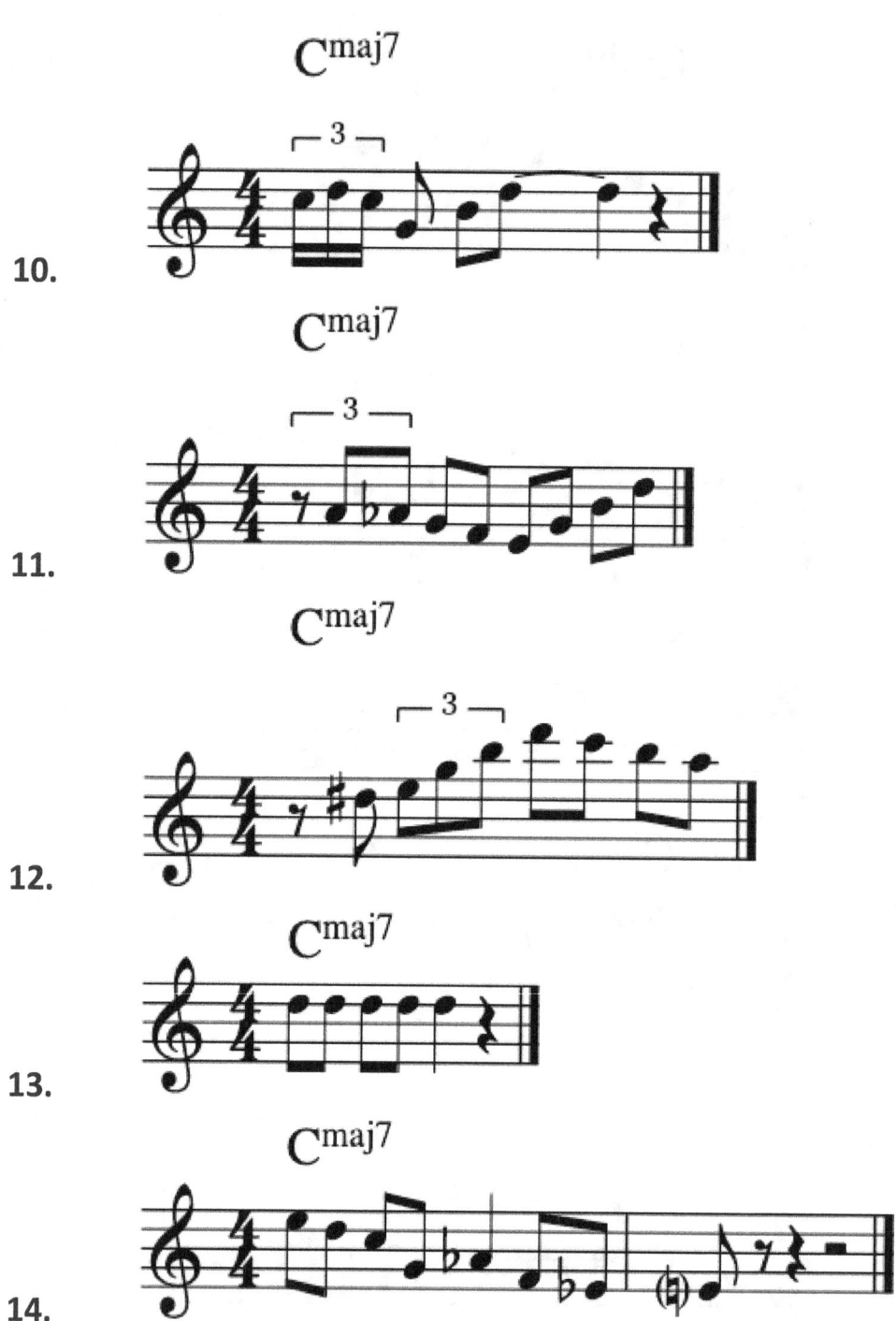

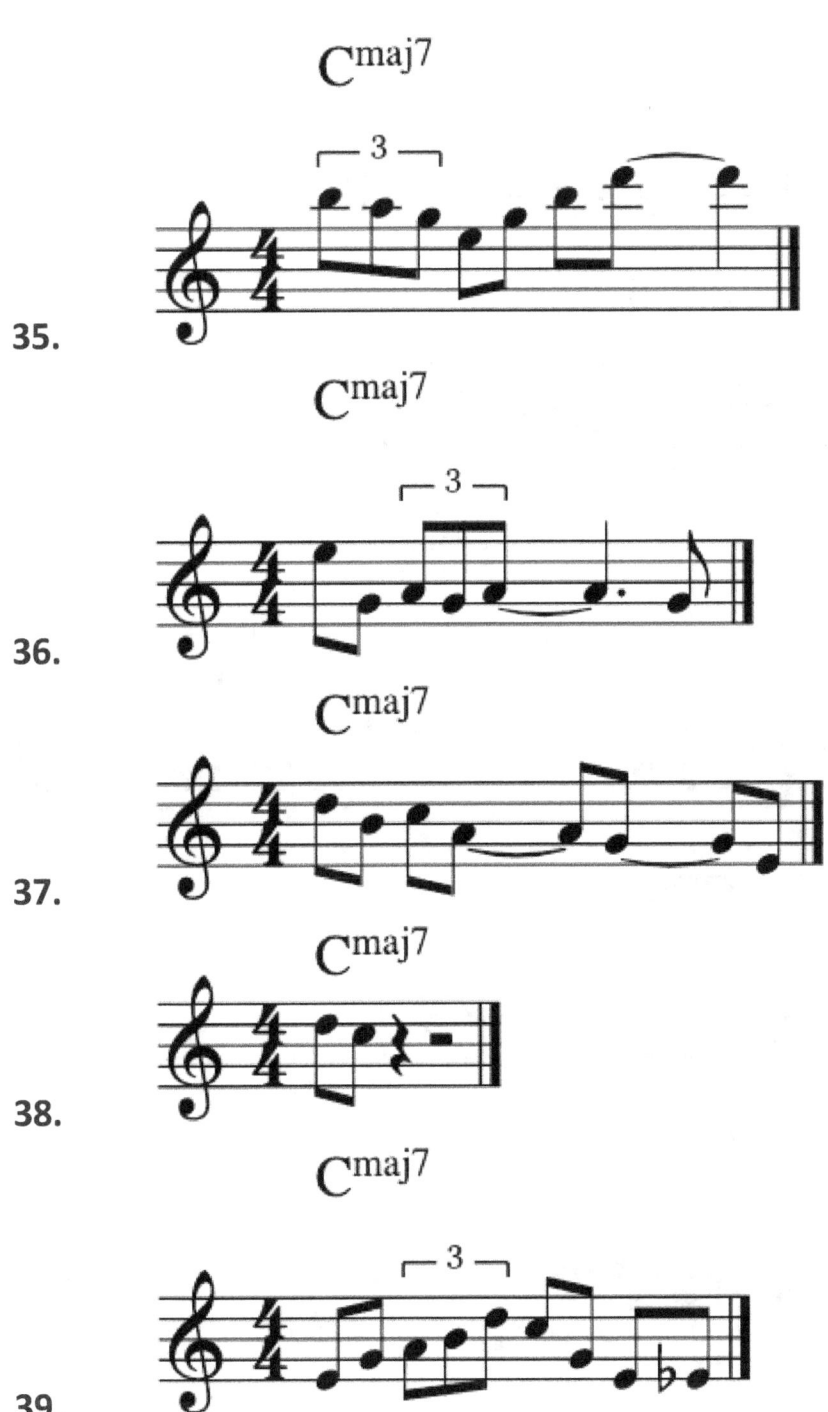

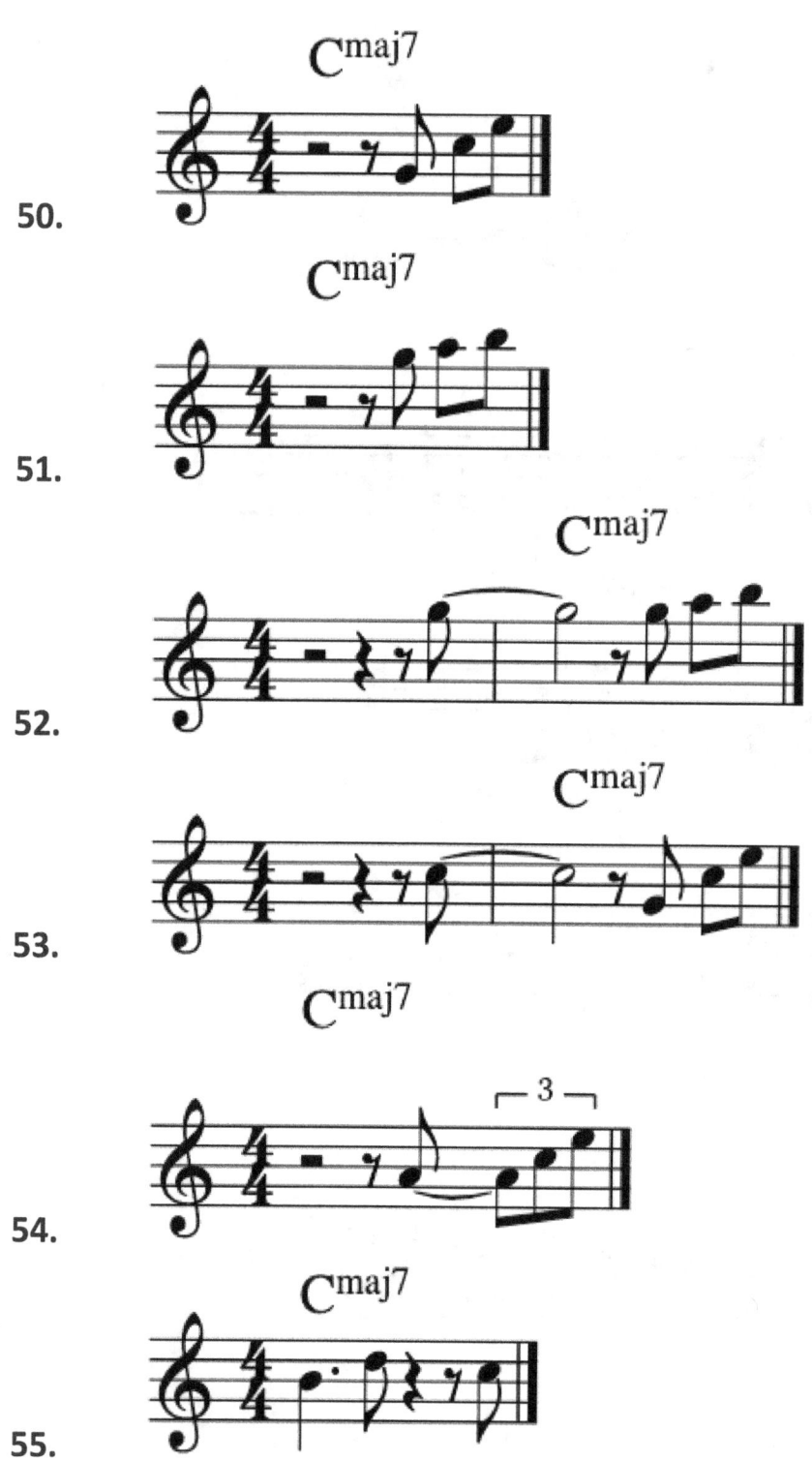

D Major

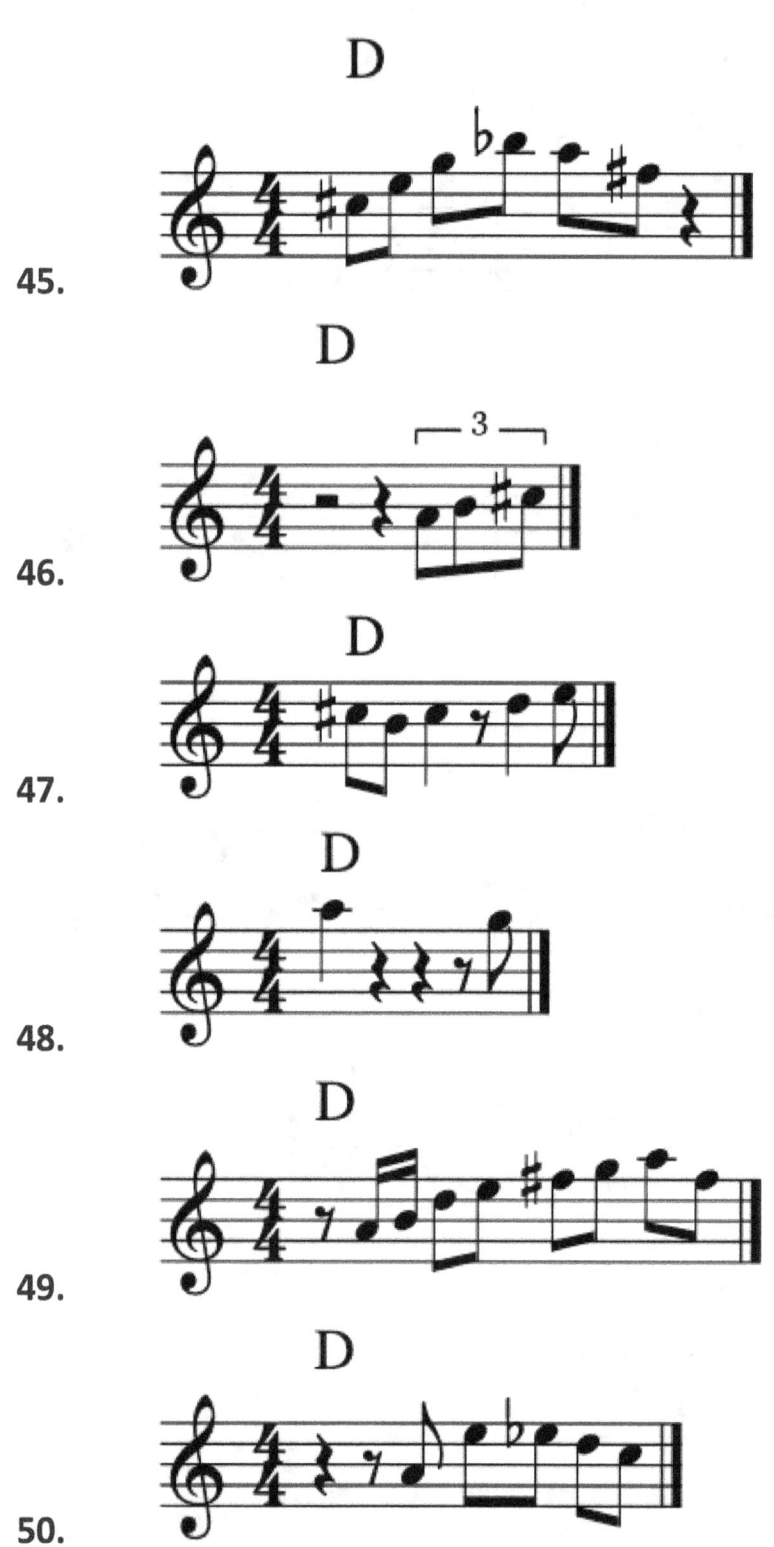

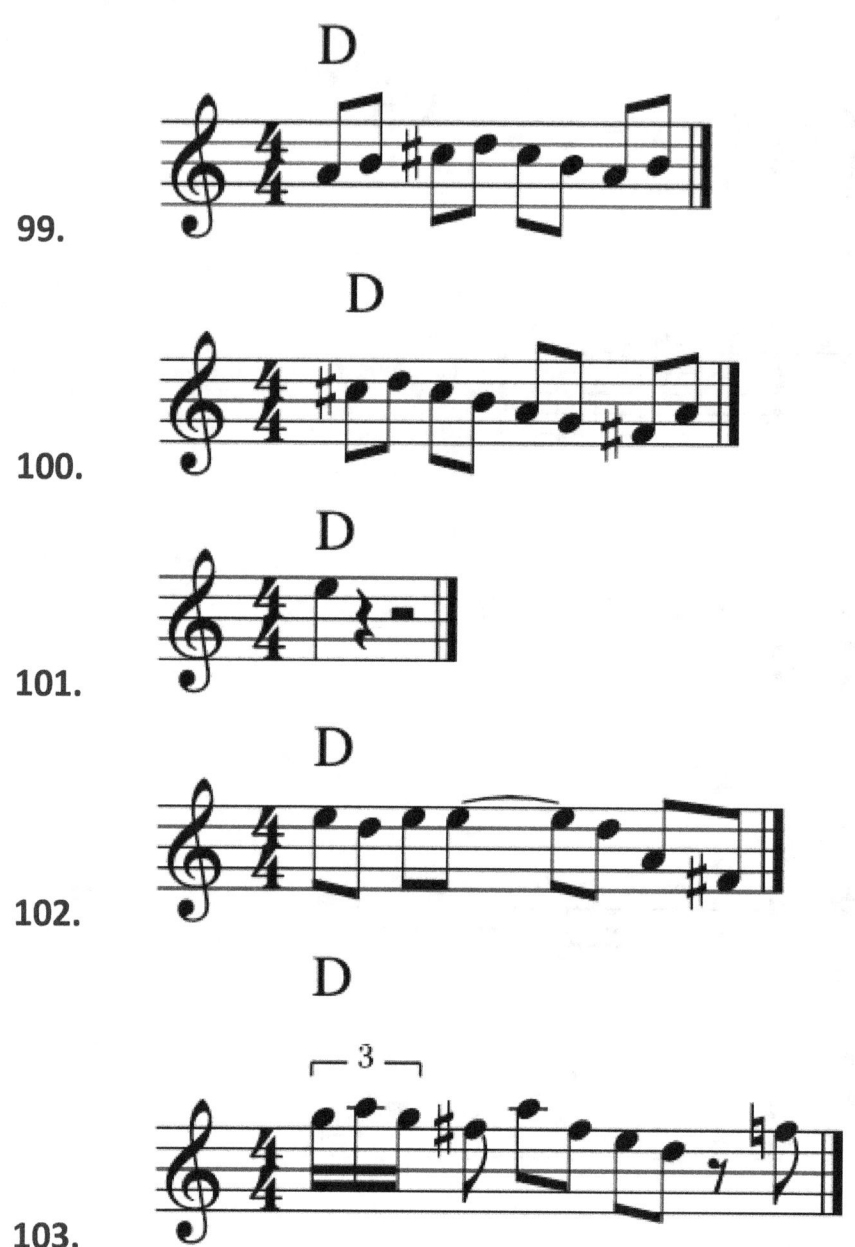

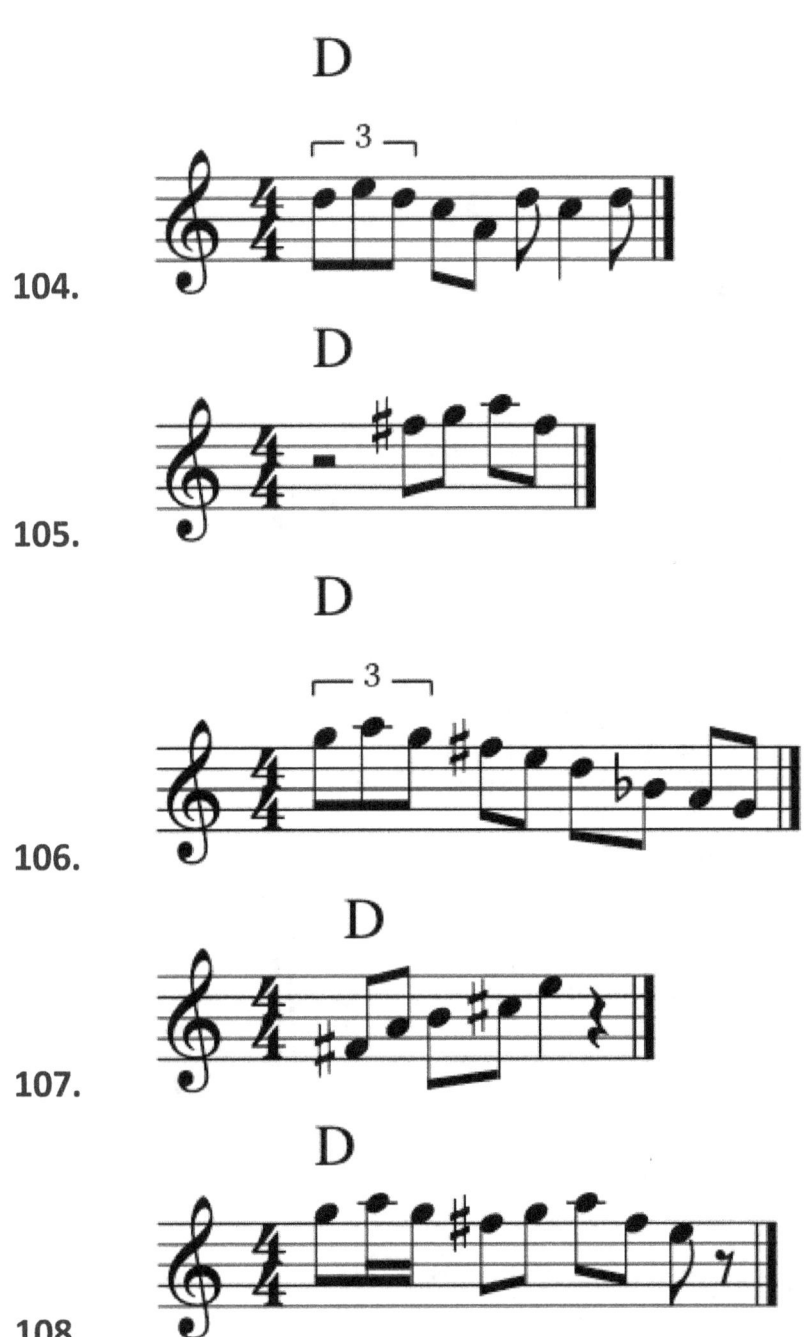

E Major

F Major

10.

11.

12.

13.

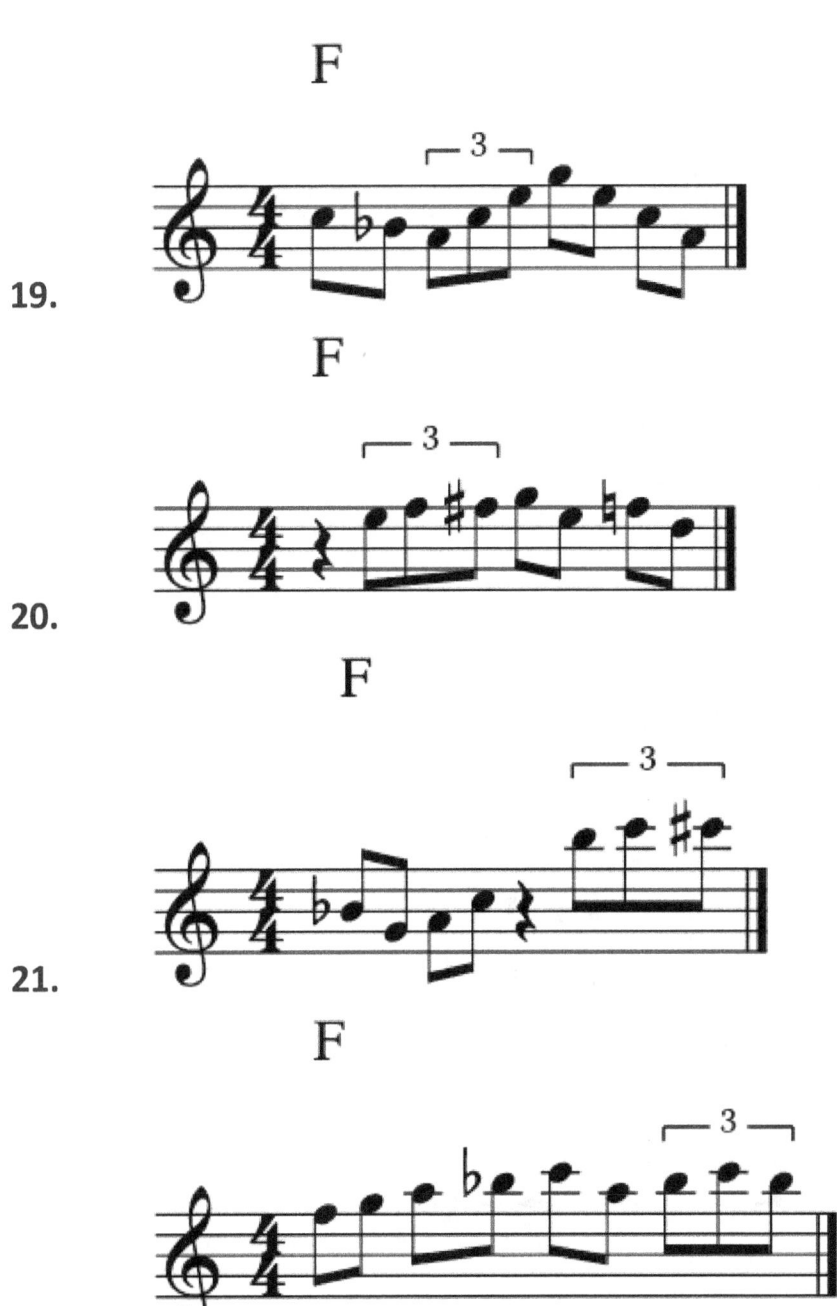

F# Major (Gb Major)

1.

2.

3.

4.

5.

6.

7.

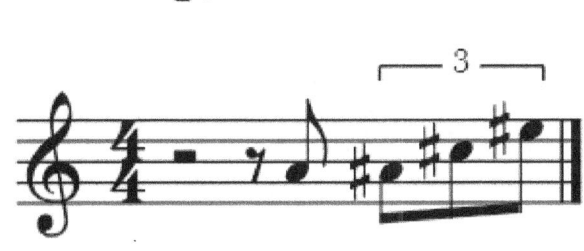

8.

G Major

20.

21.

22.

23.

24.

30.

31.

32.

33.

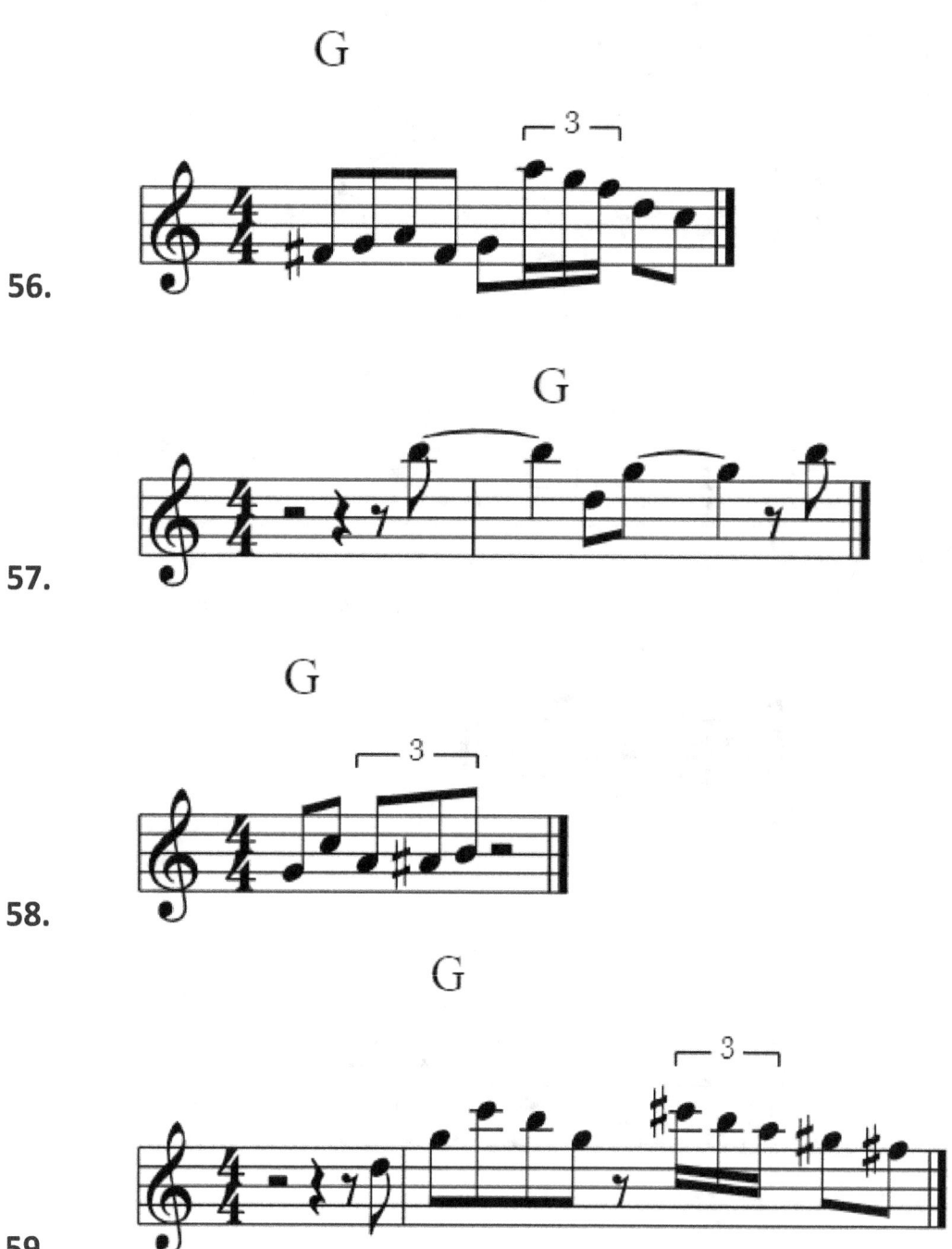

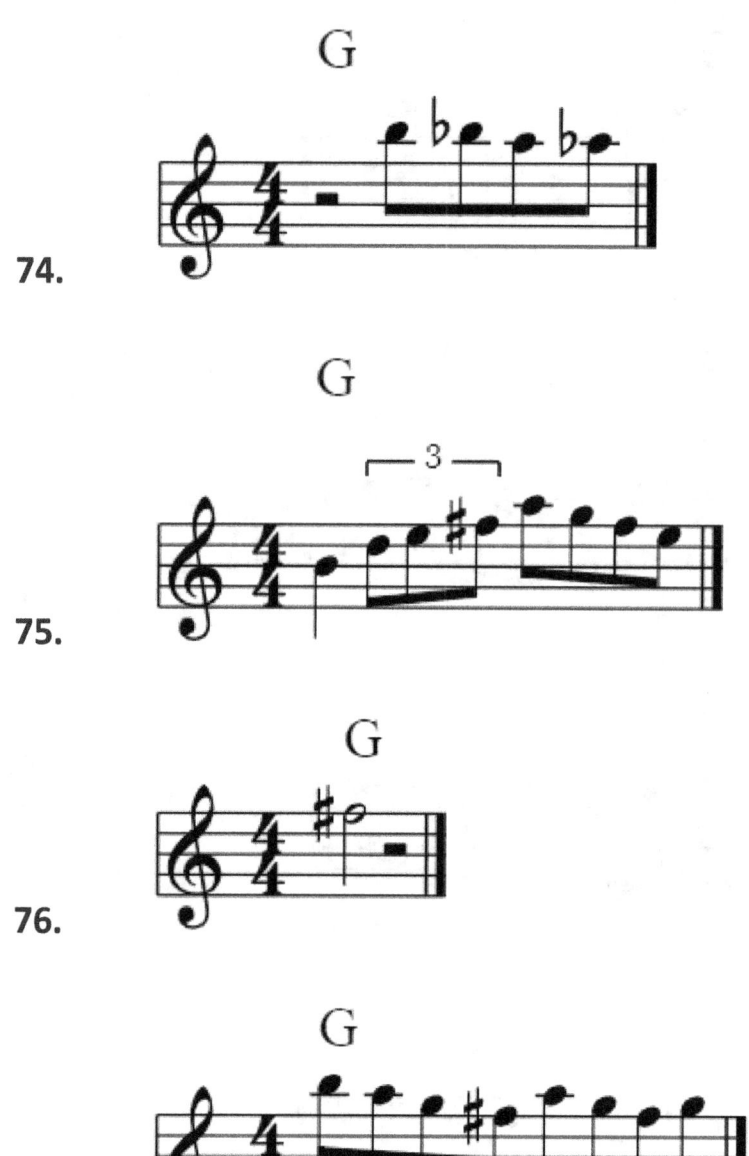

83.

84.

85.

86.

87.

116.

117.

118.

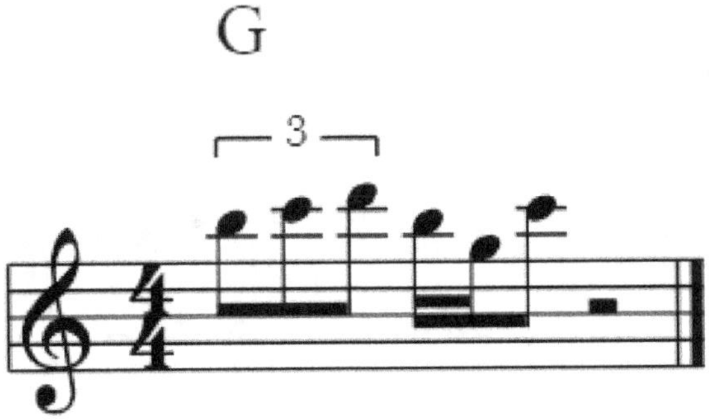

119.

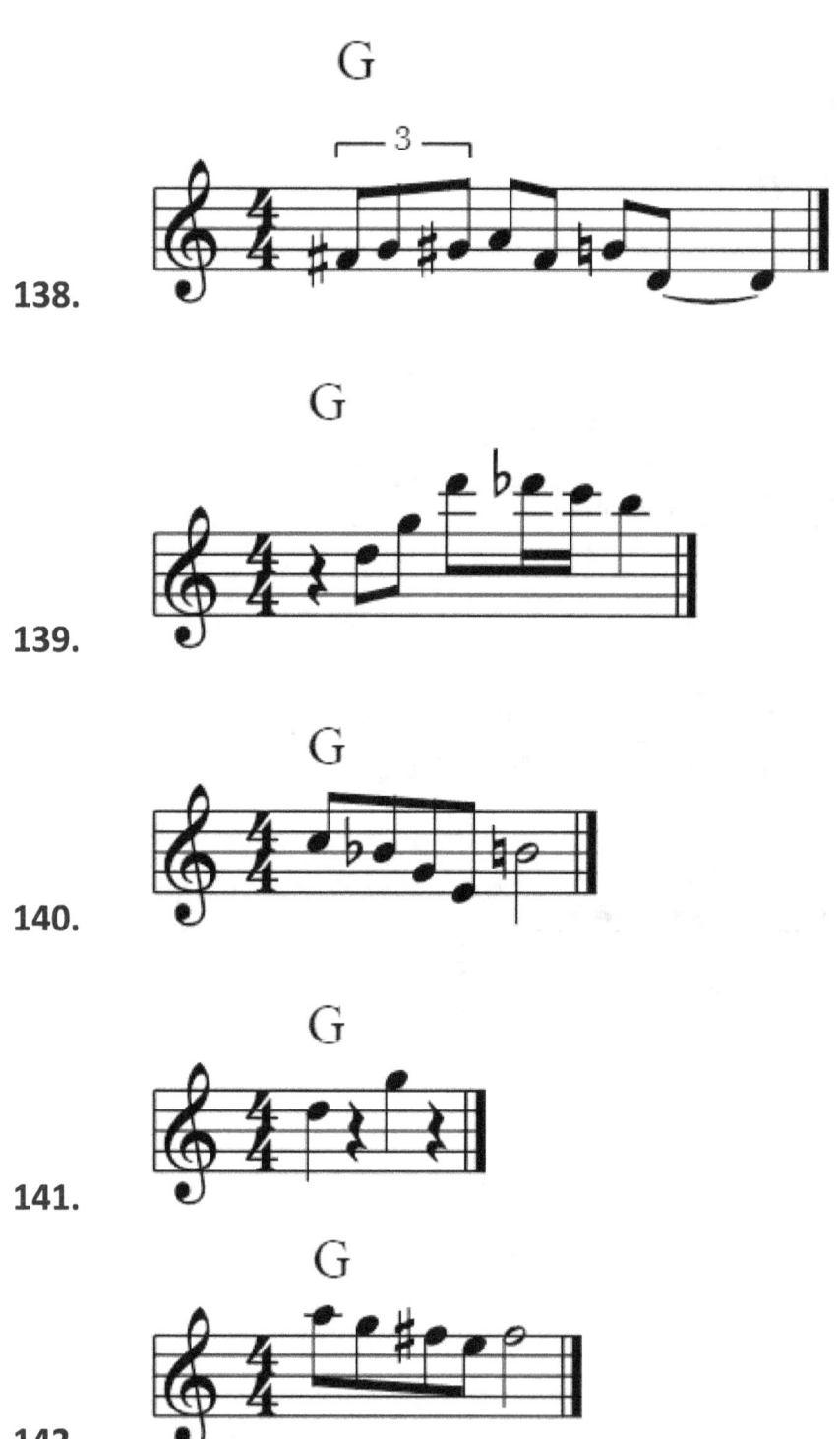

143.

144.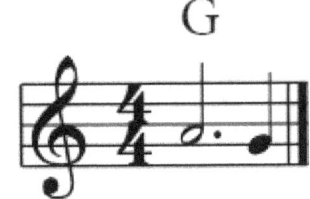

145.

146.

147.

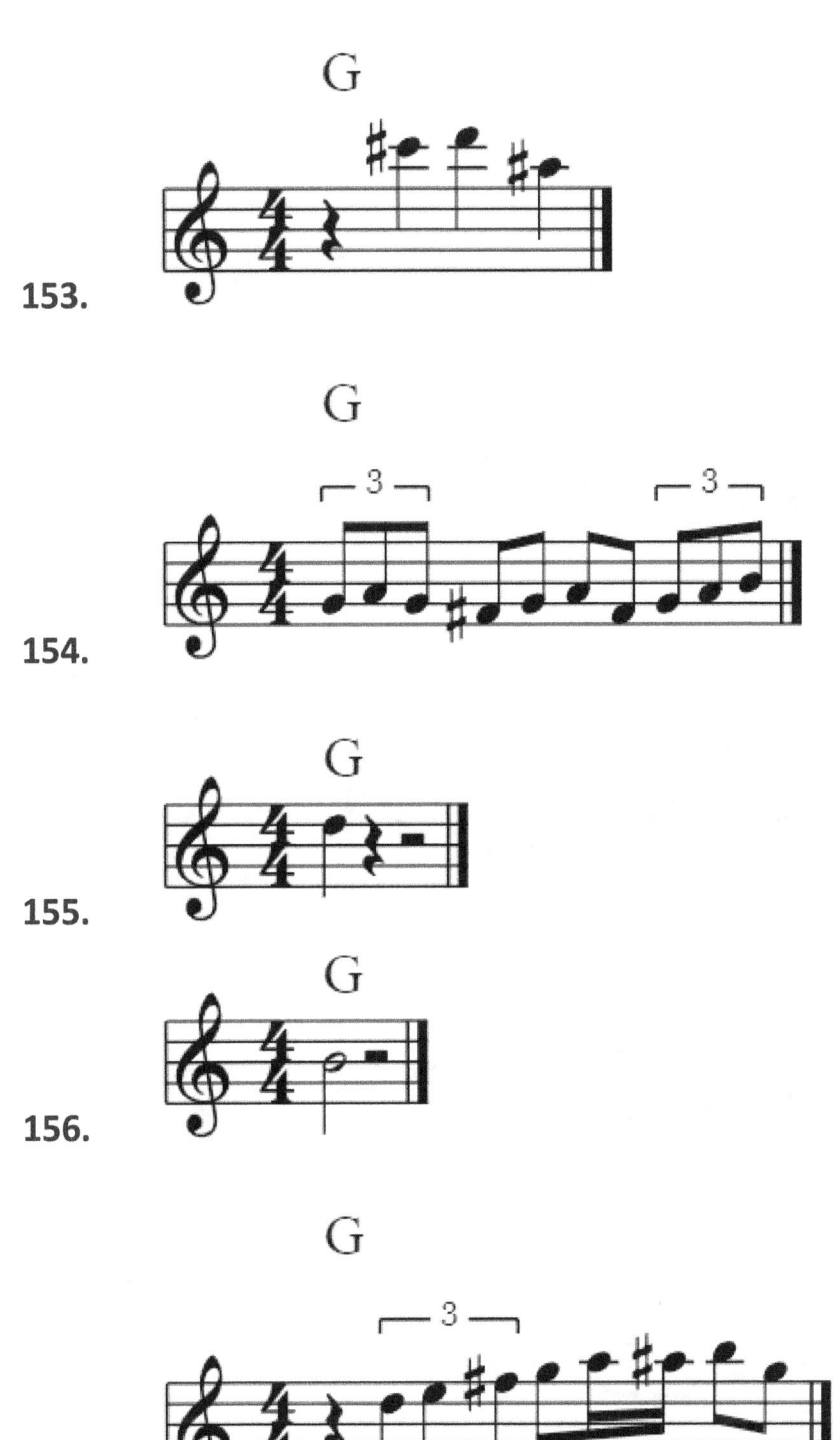

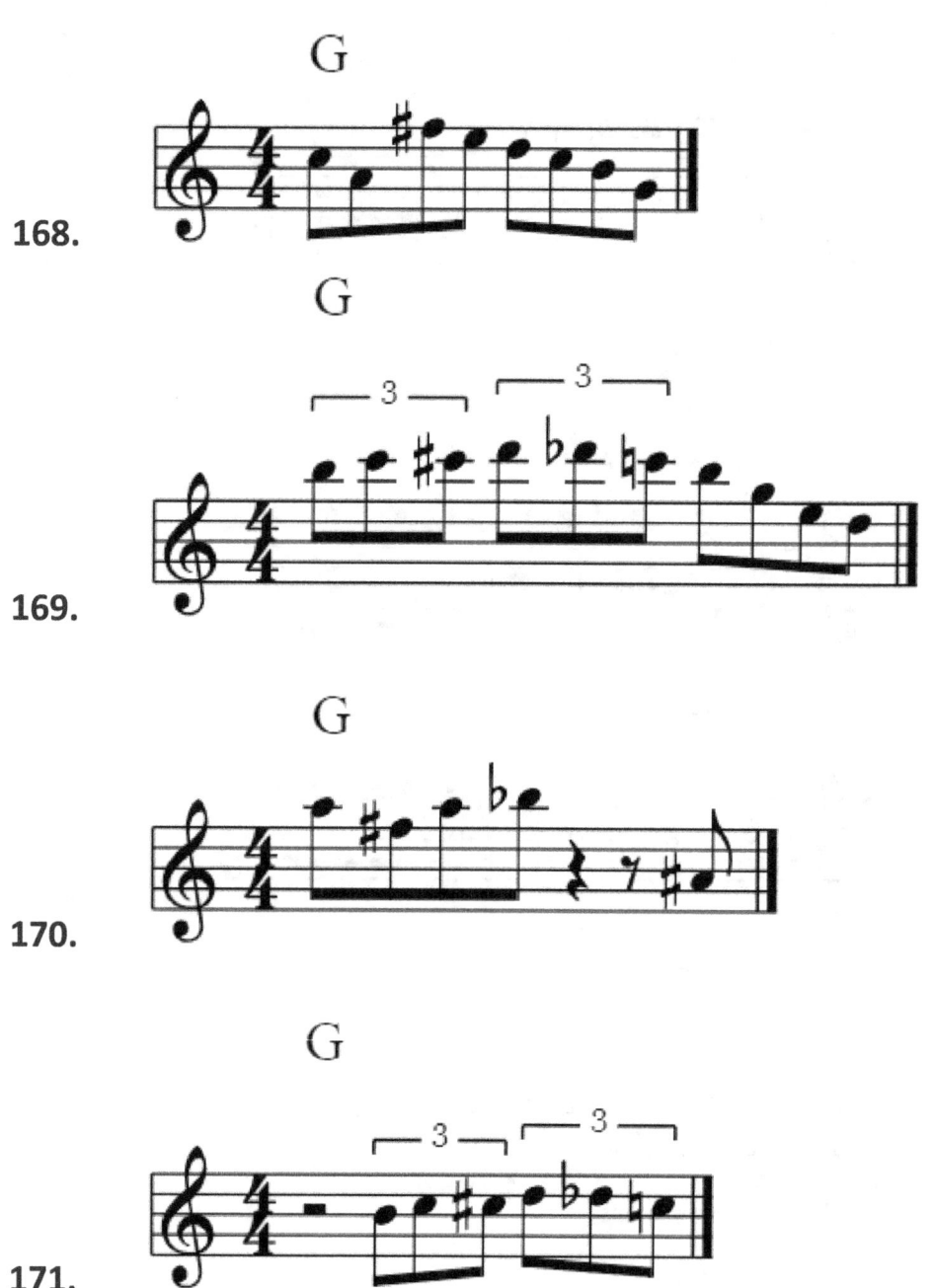

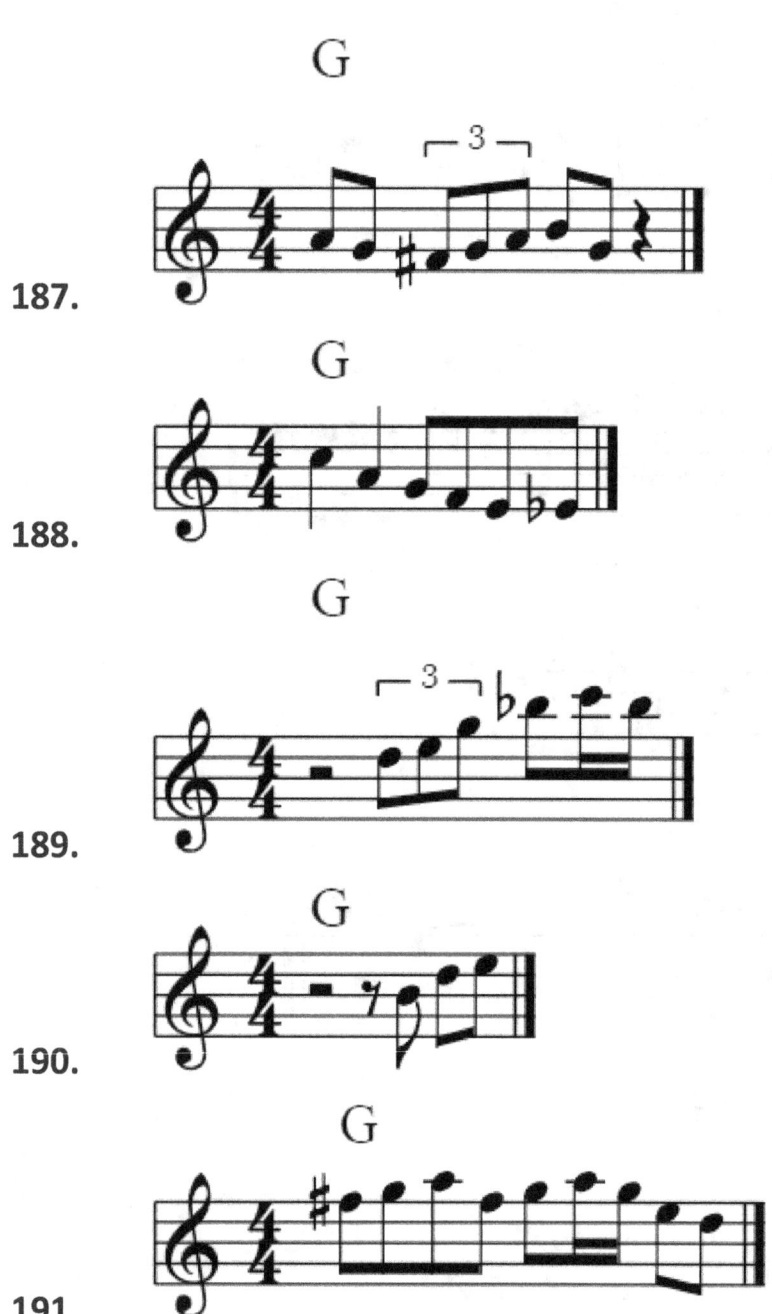

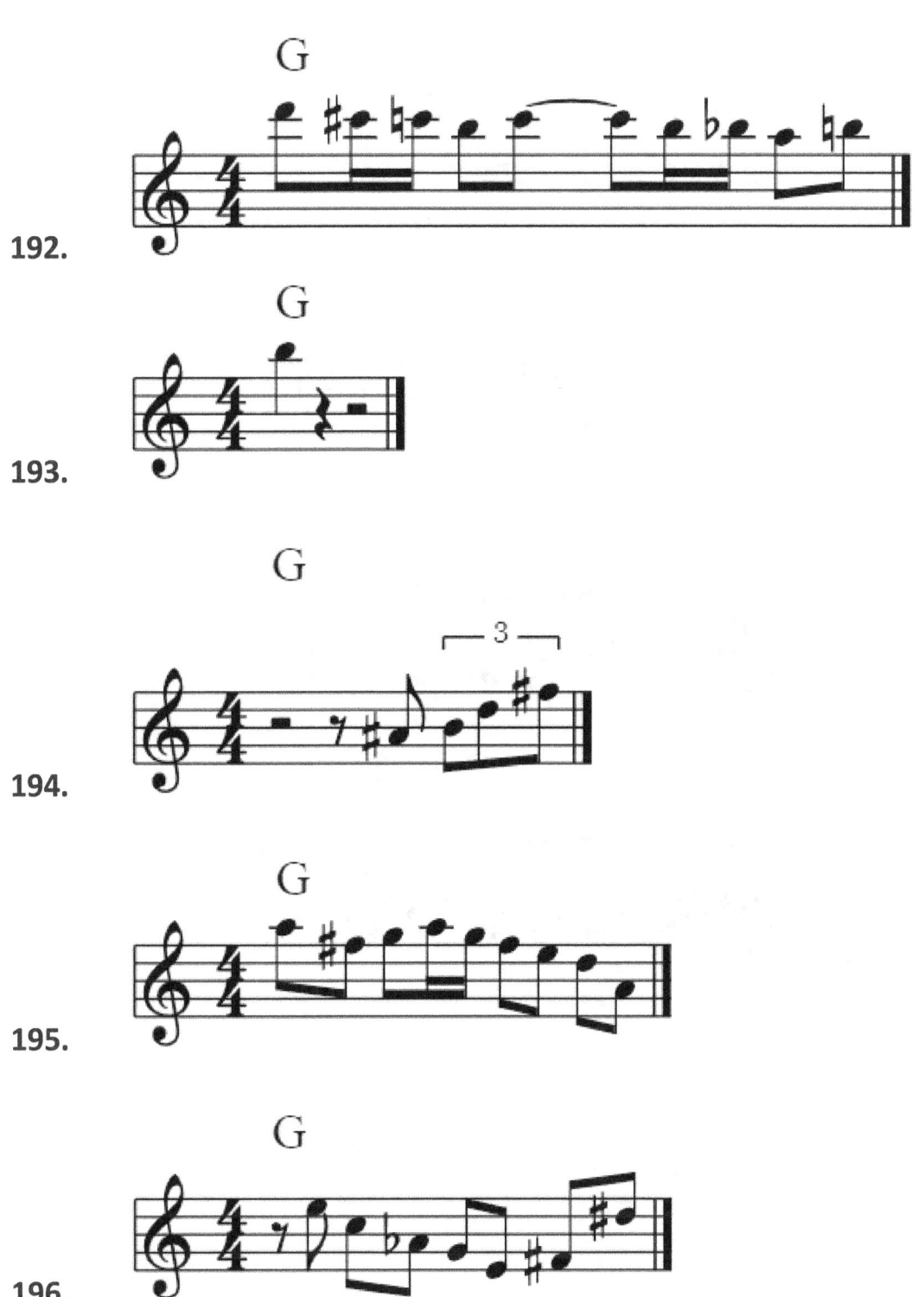

212.

213.

214.

215.

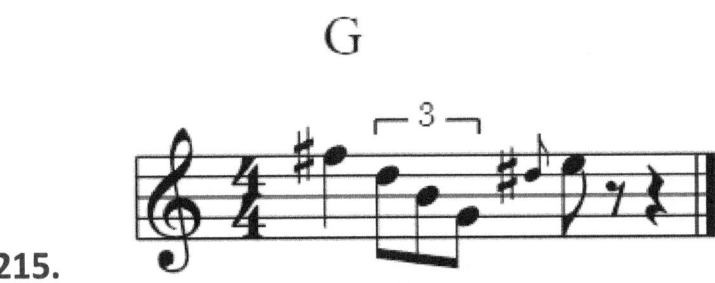

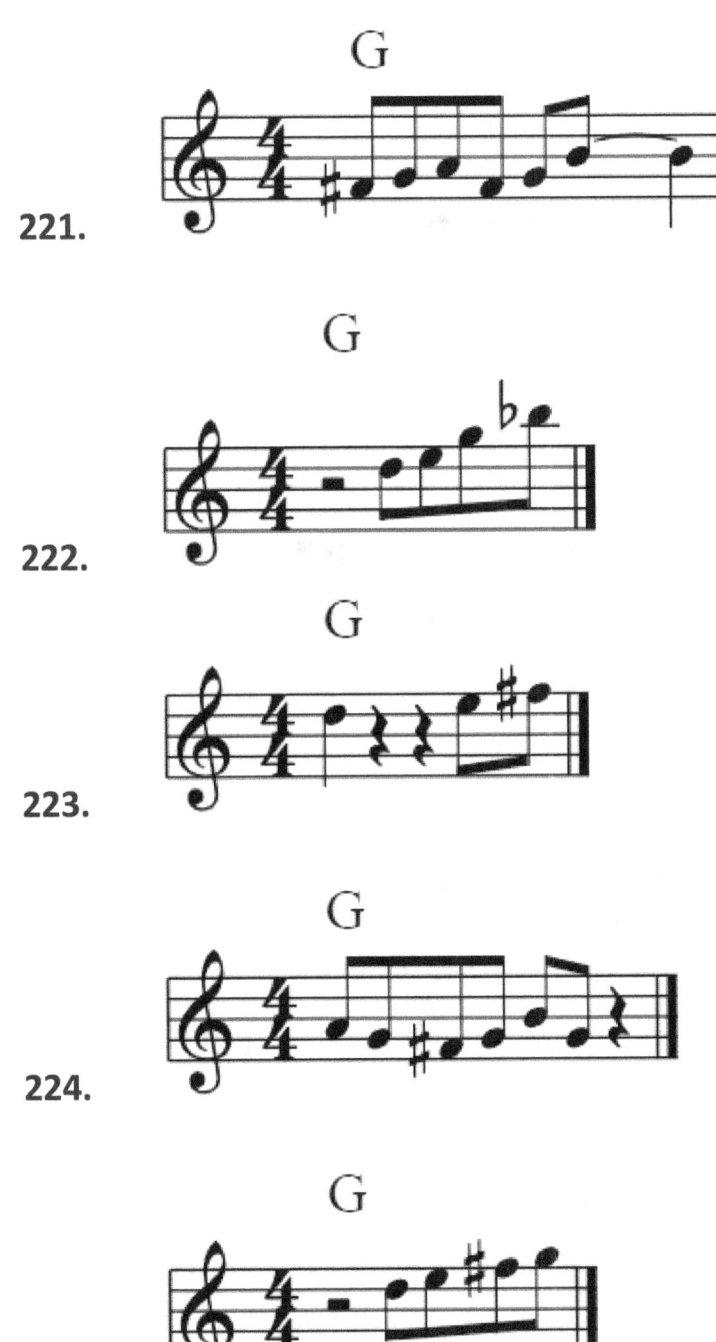

230.

231.

232.

233.

238.

239.

240.

241.

242.

243.
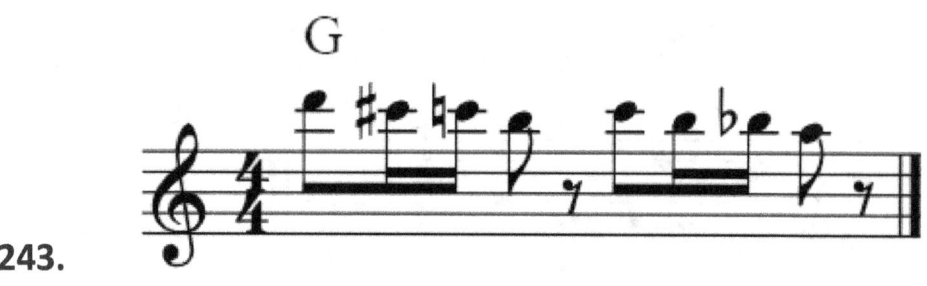

244.

245.

246.

247.

G

248.

G

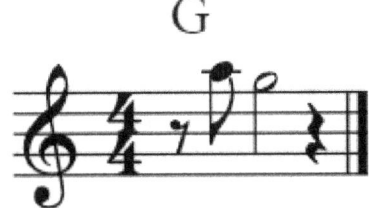

249.

G

250.

G

251.

252.

253.

254.

255.

256.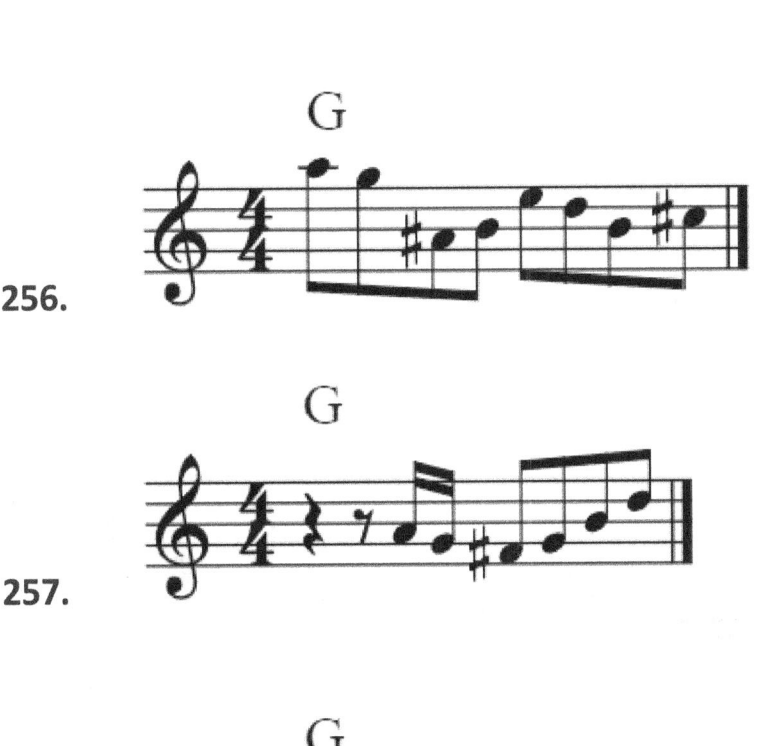

257.

258.

259.

260.

Major Progressions:

Major to Major:

C to Ab

1.

Major to Dominant 7:

C to A7

1.

2.

3.

C to C7

4.

D to B7

1.

2.

3.

D to G7

6.

7.

F to D7

1.

F to F7

G to E7

13.

14.

15.

16.

Major to Dominant 7b9:

A to F#7b9

1.

G to E7b9

1.

2.

Major to Minor:

Bb to Bb min

C to C min

G to Bb min

Major to Minor to Dominant 7:
C to B min to E7

1.

Major to Fully Diminished:
A to C 0 (Fully Diminished)

1.

C to C# 07 (Fully Diminished)

Chapter #2

Dominant 7 Chords and Progressions

Dominant 7 Chords:

Ab7

1.

2.

3.

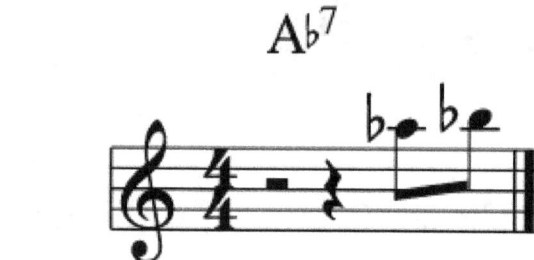

A7

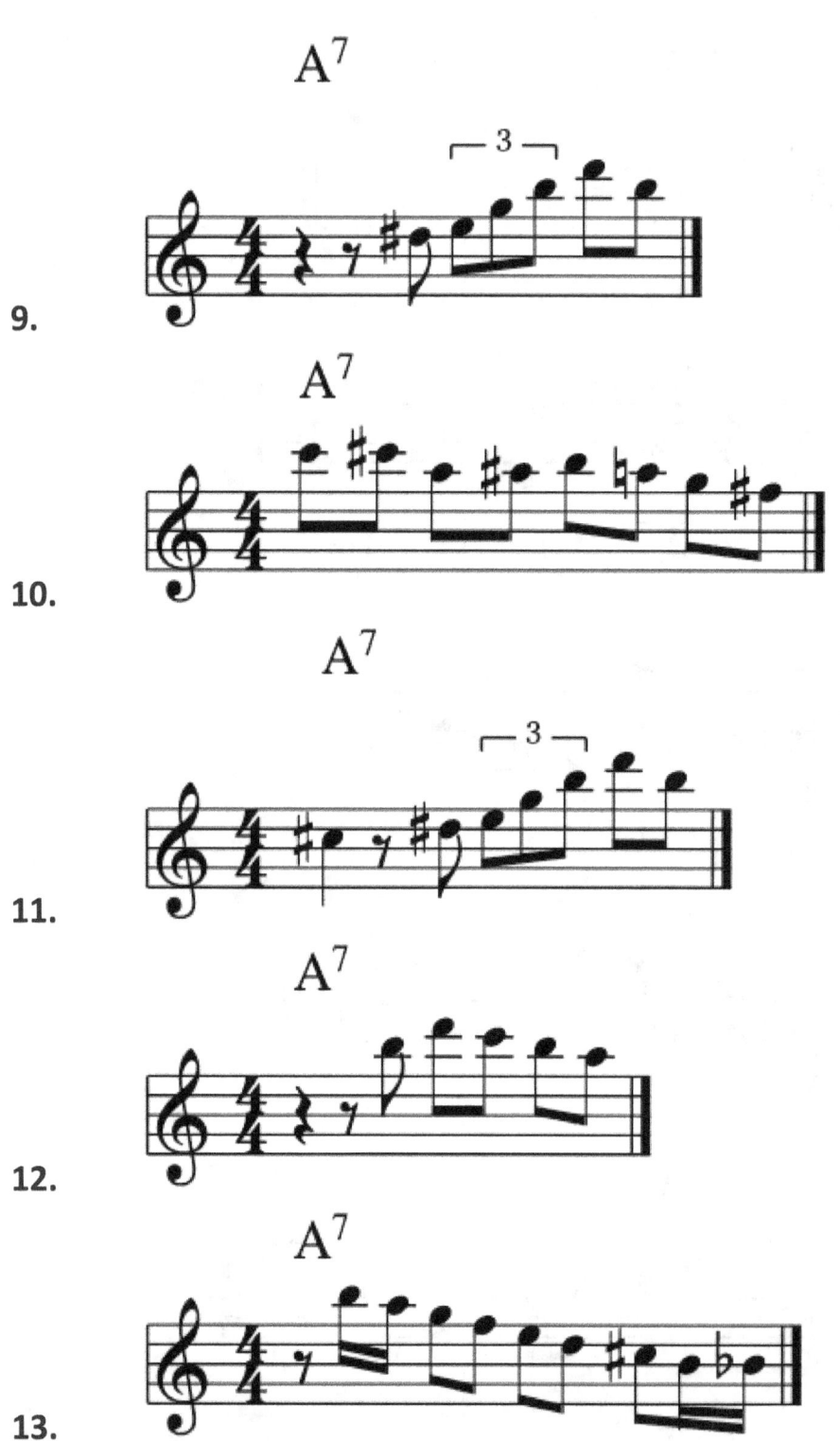

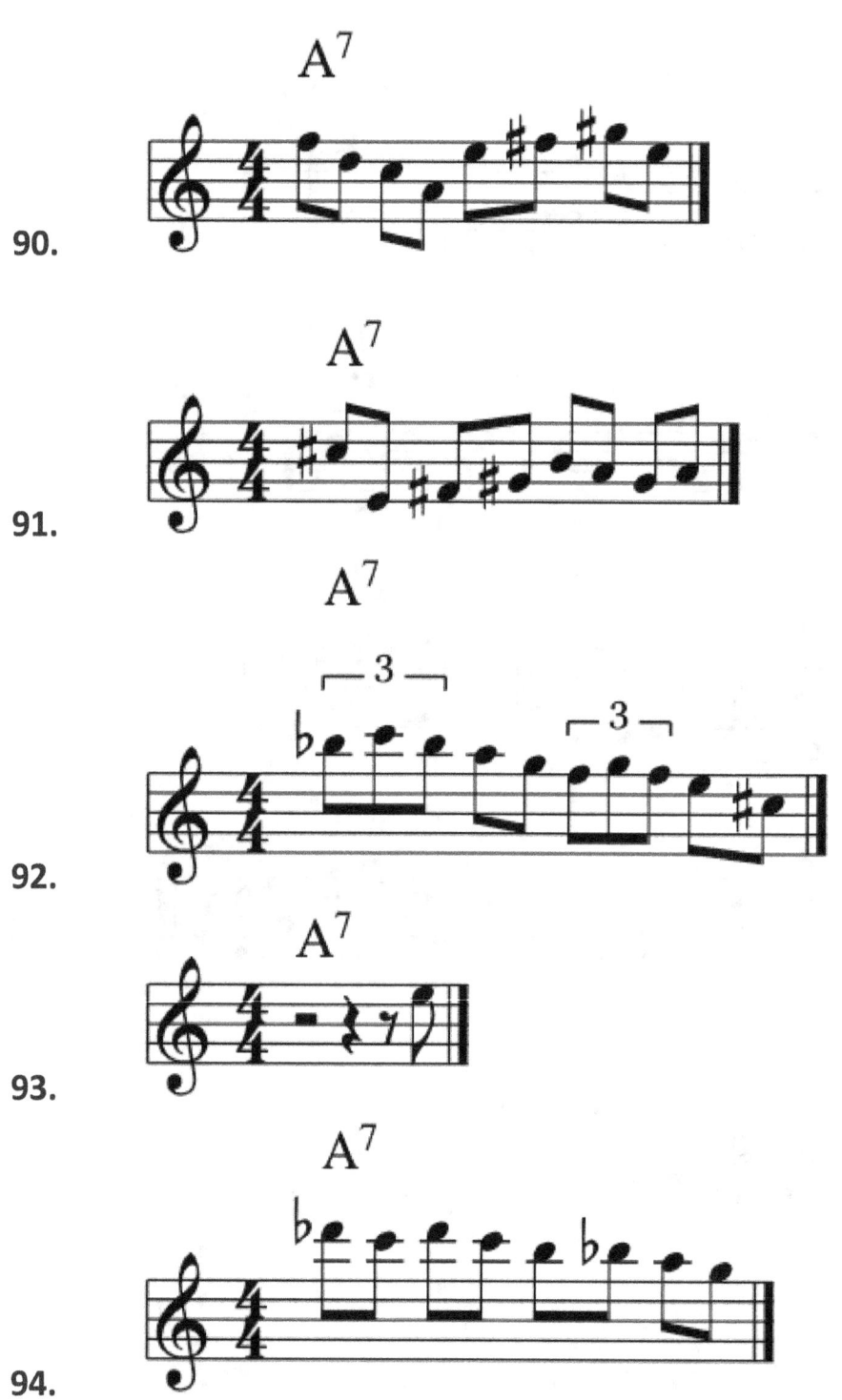

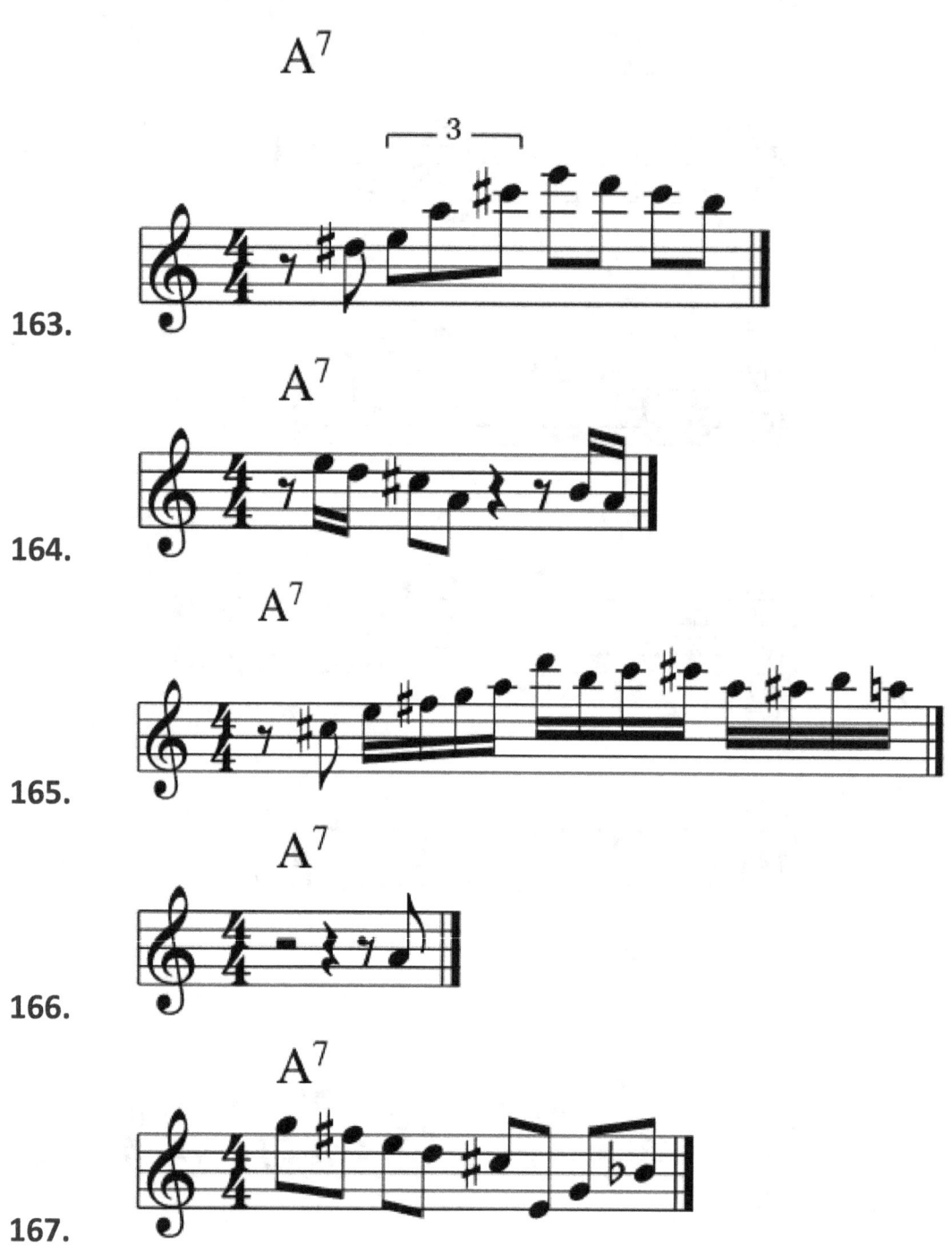

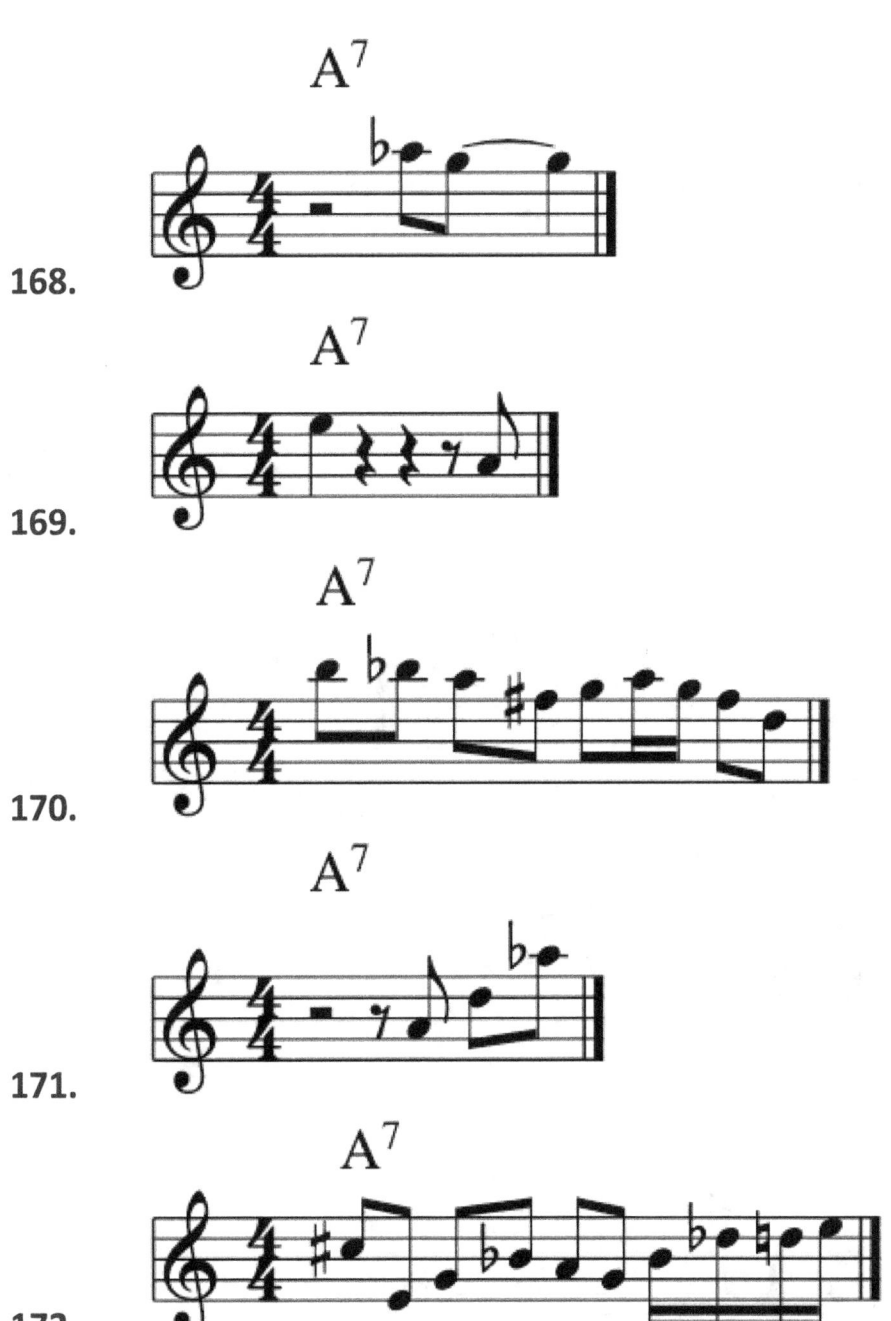

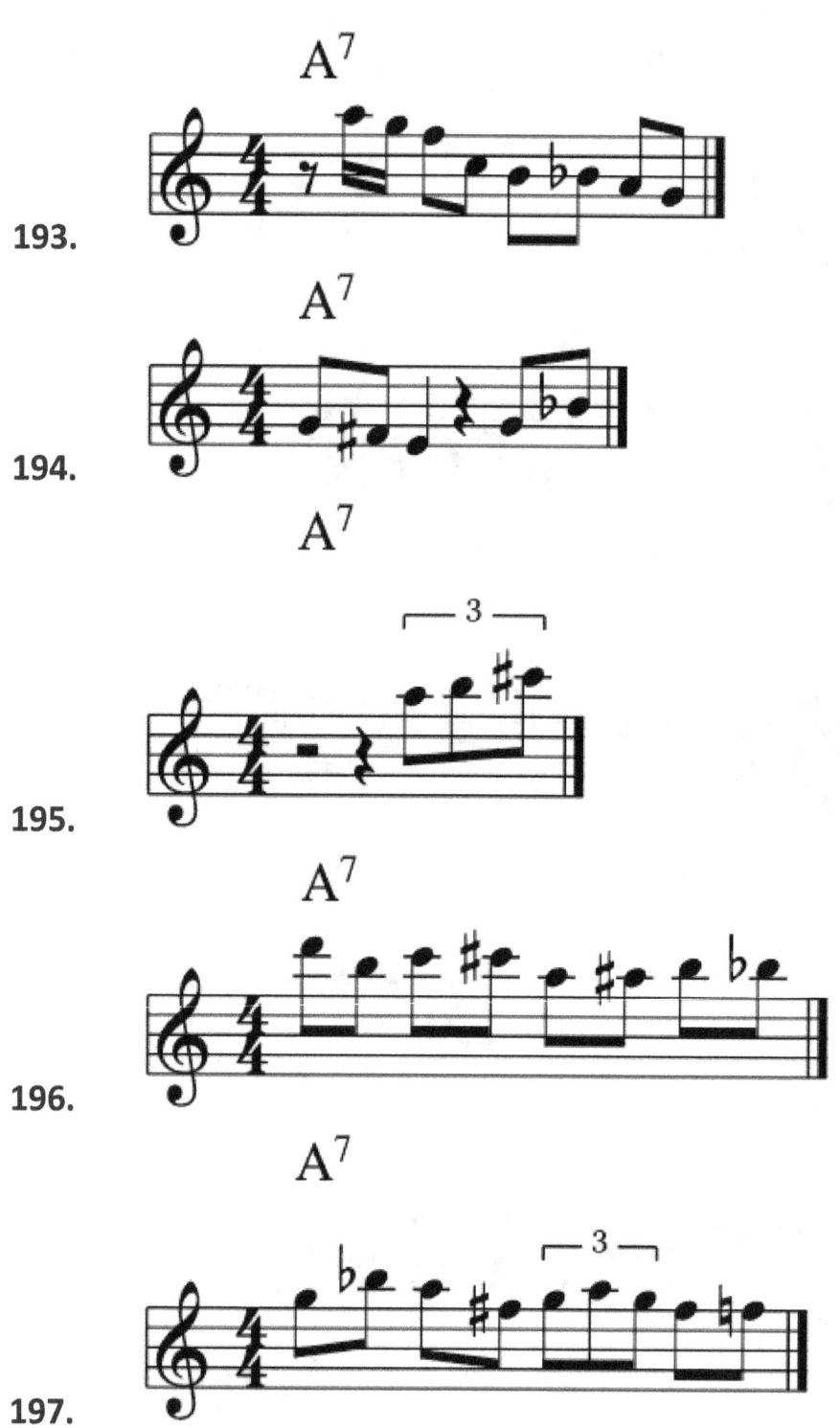

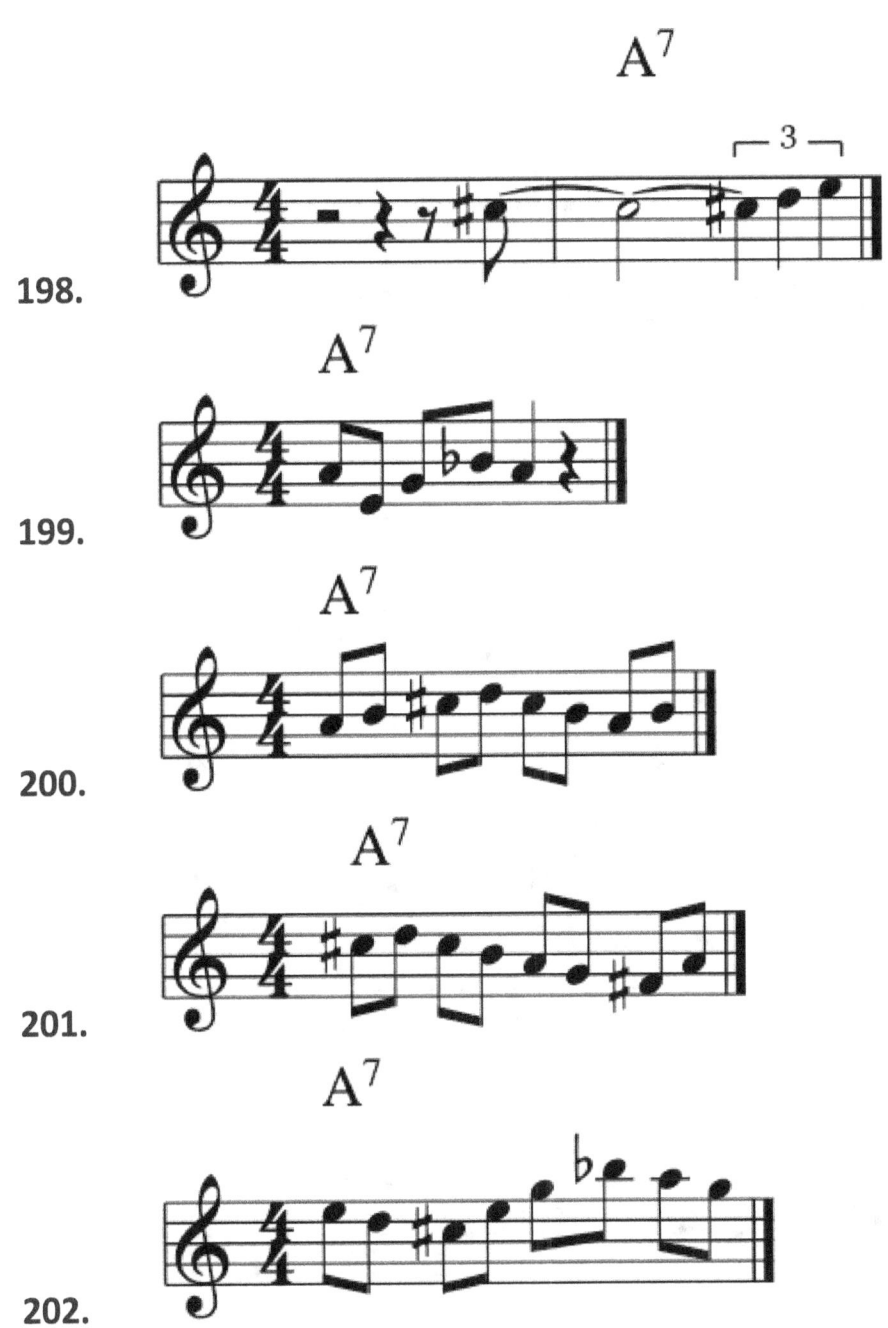

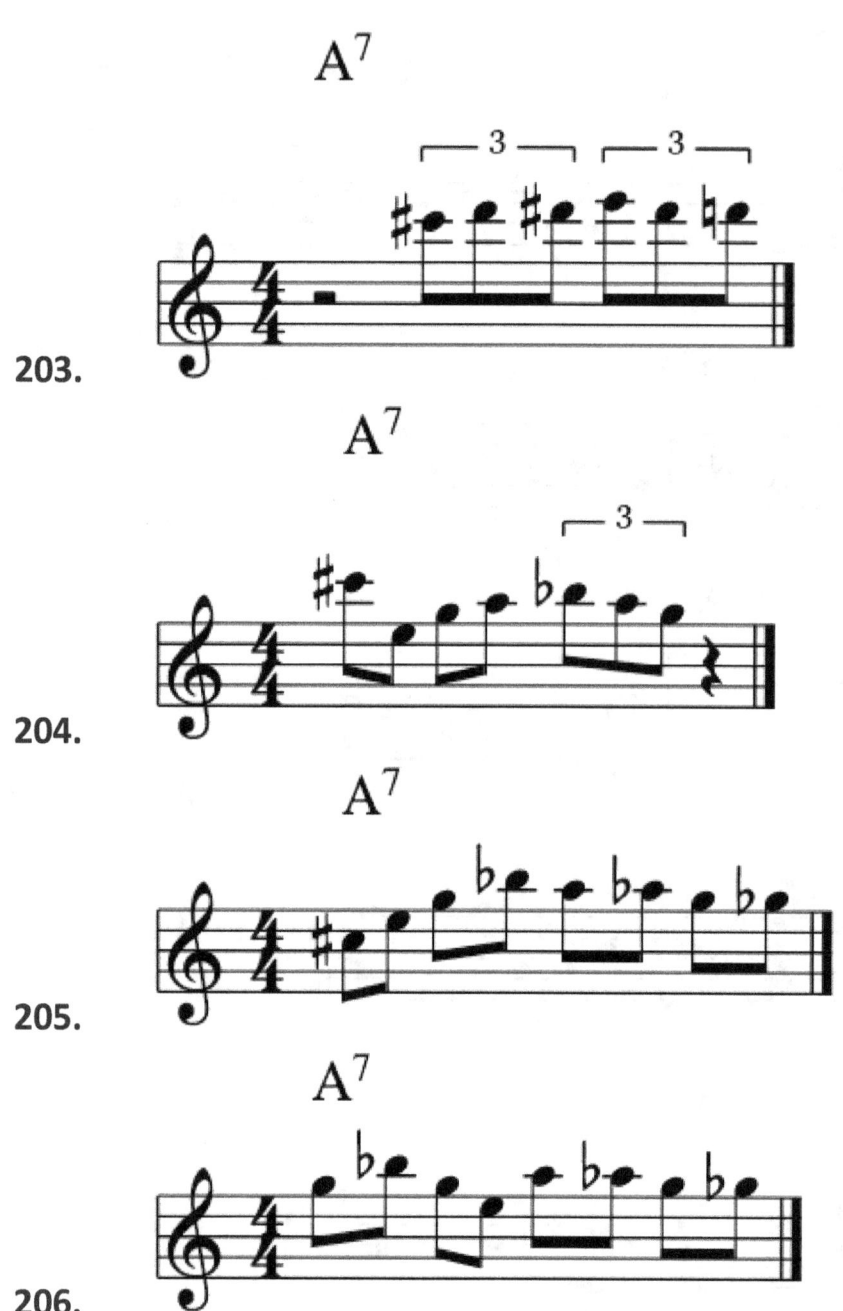

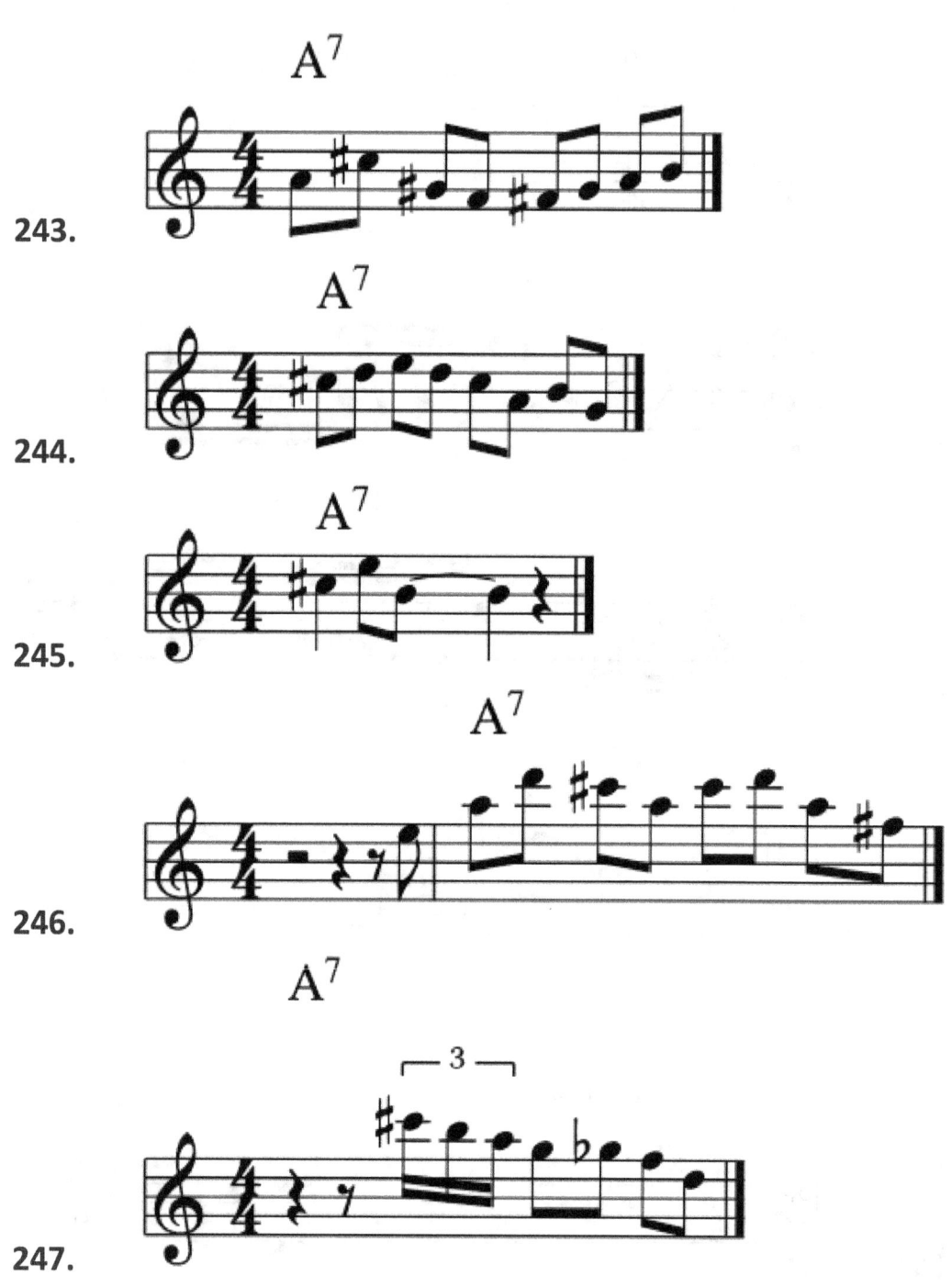

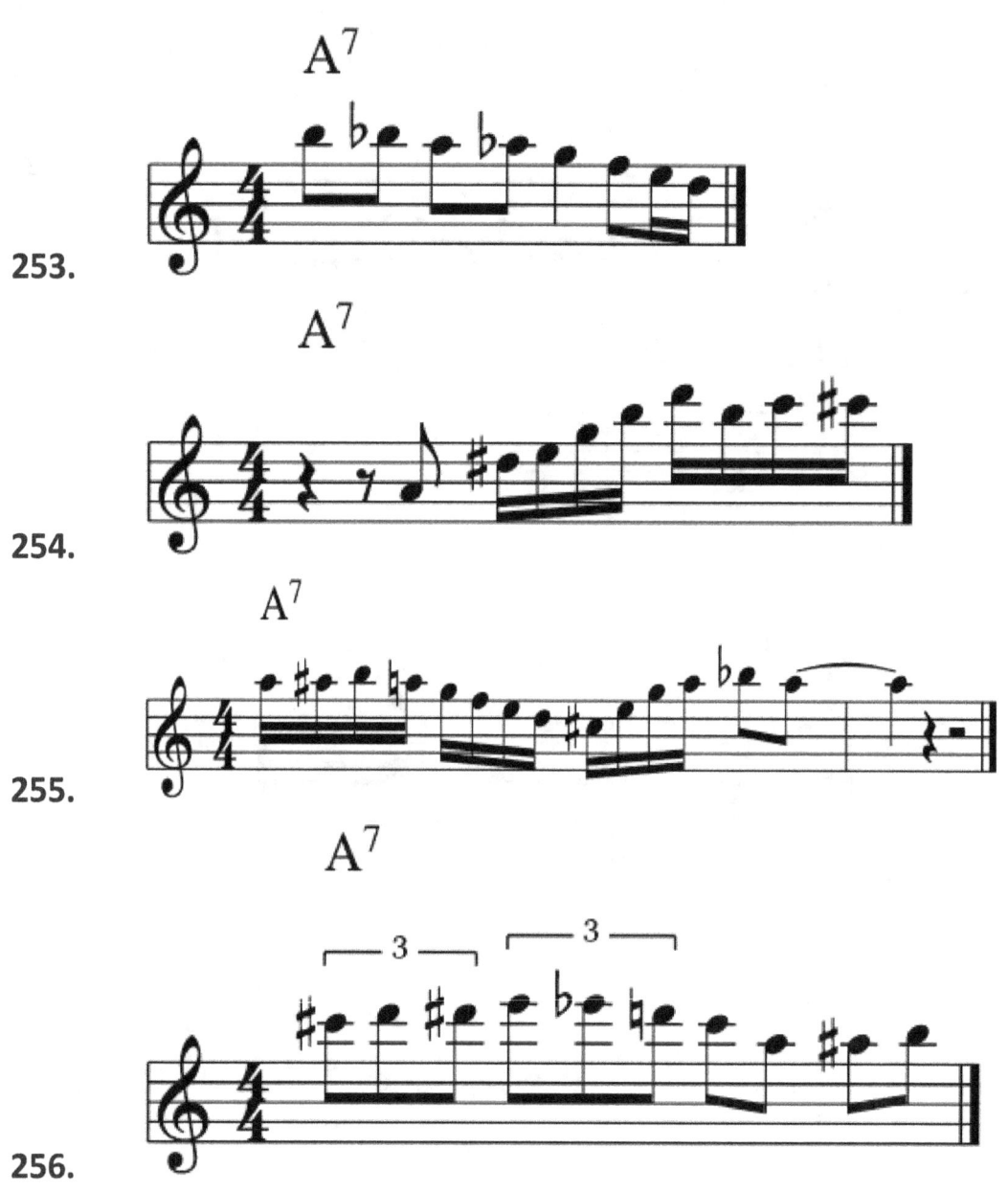

Bb7

B7

C7

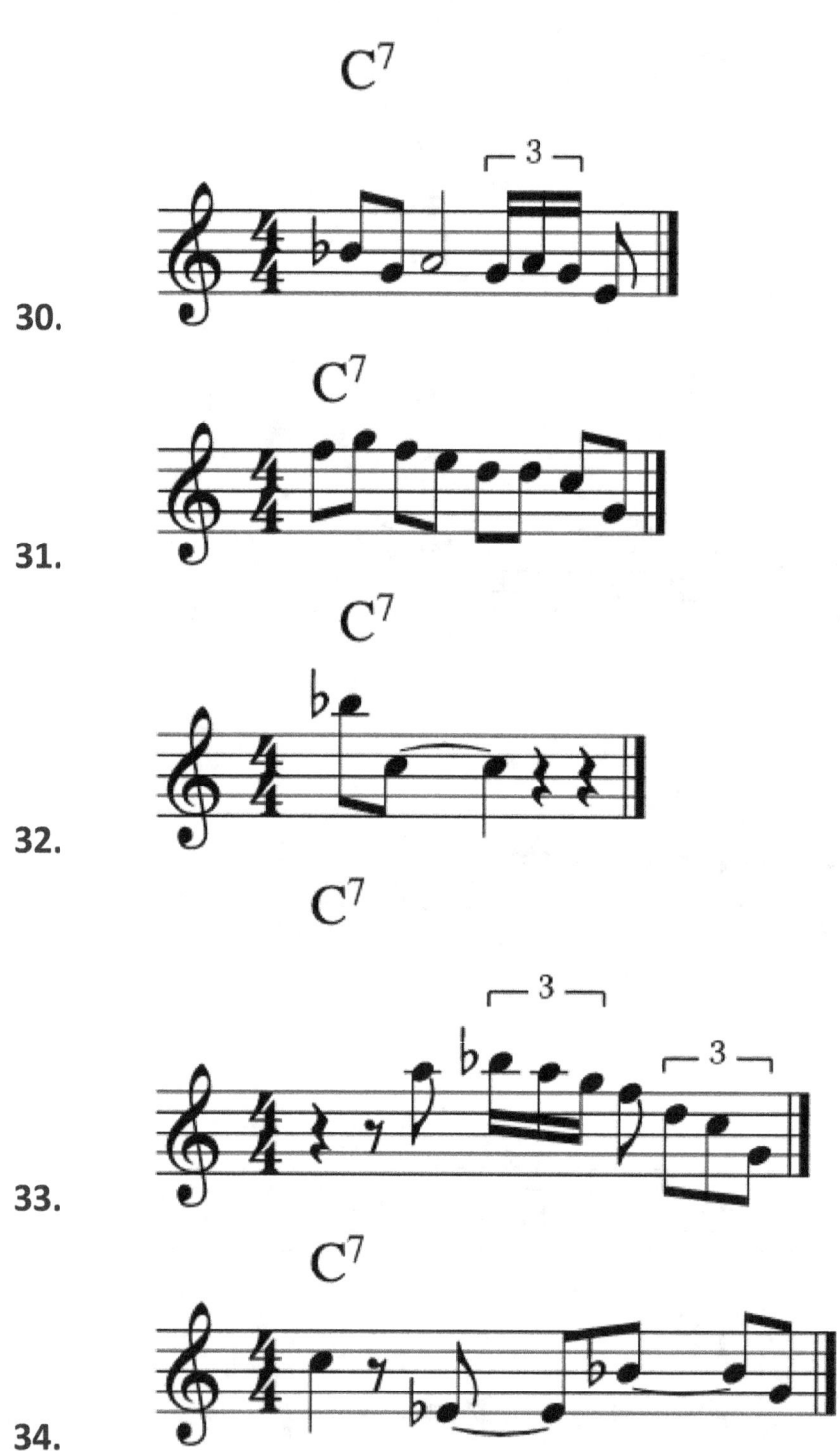

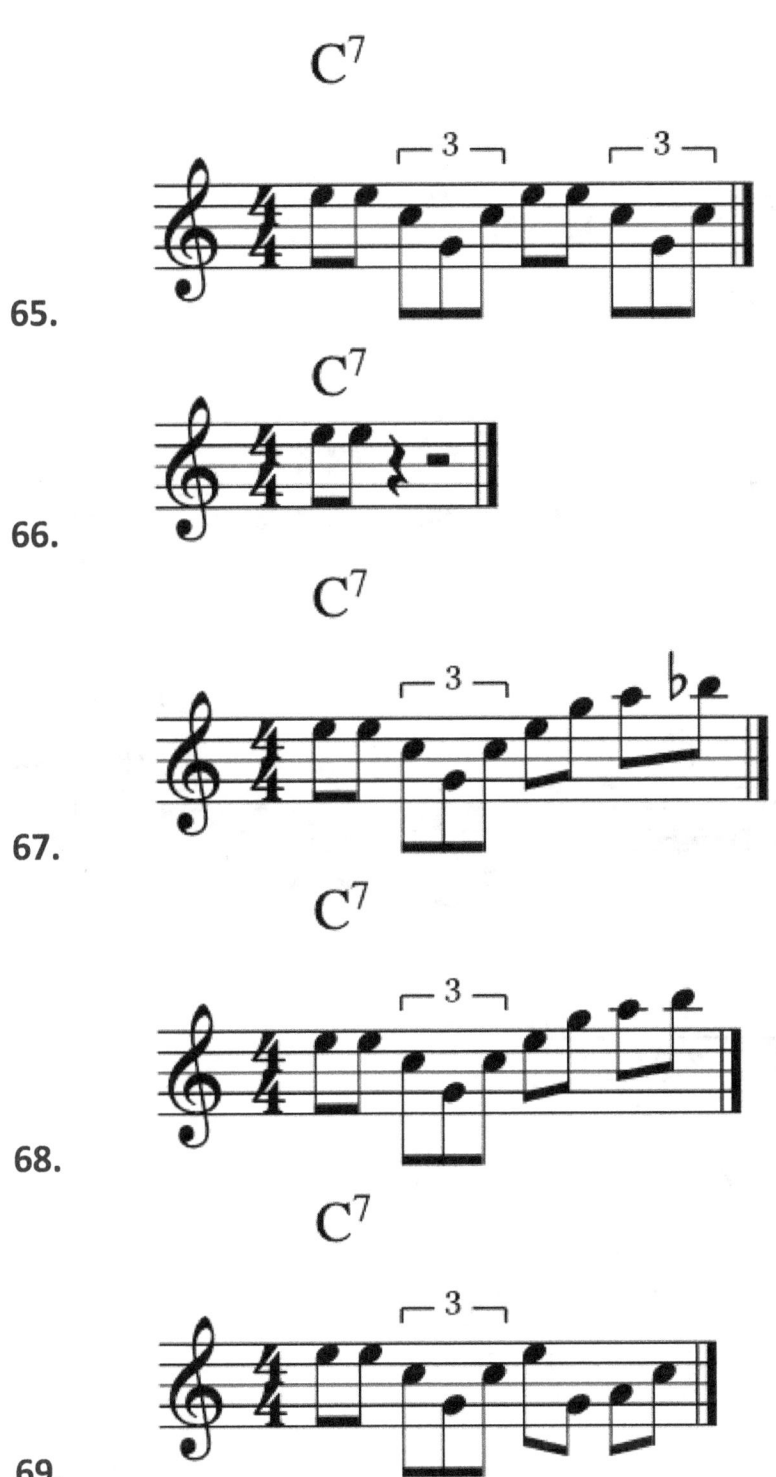

C#7 (Db7)

D7

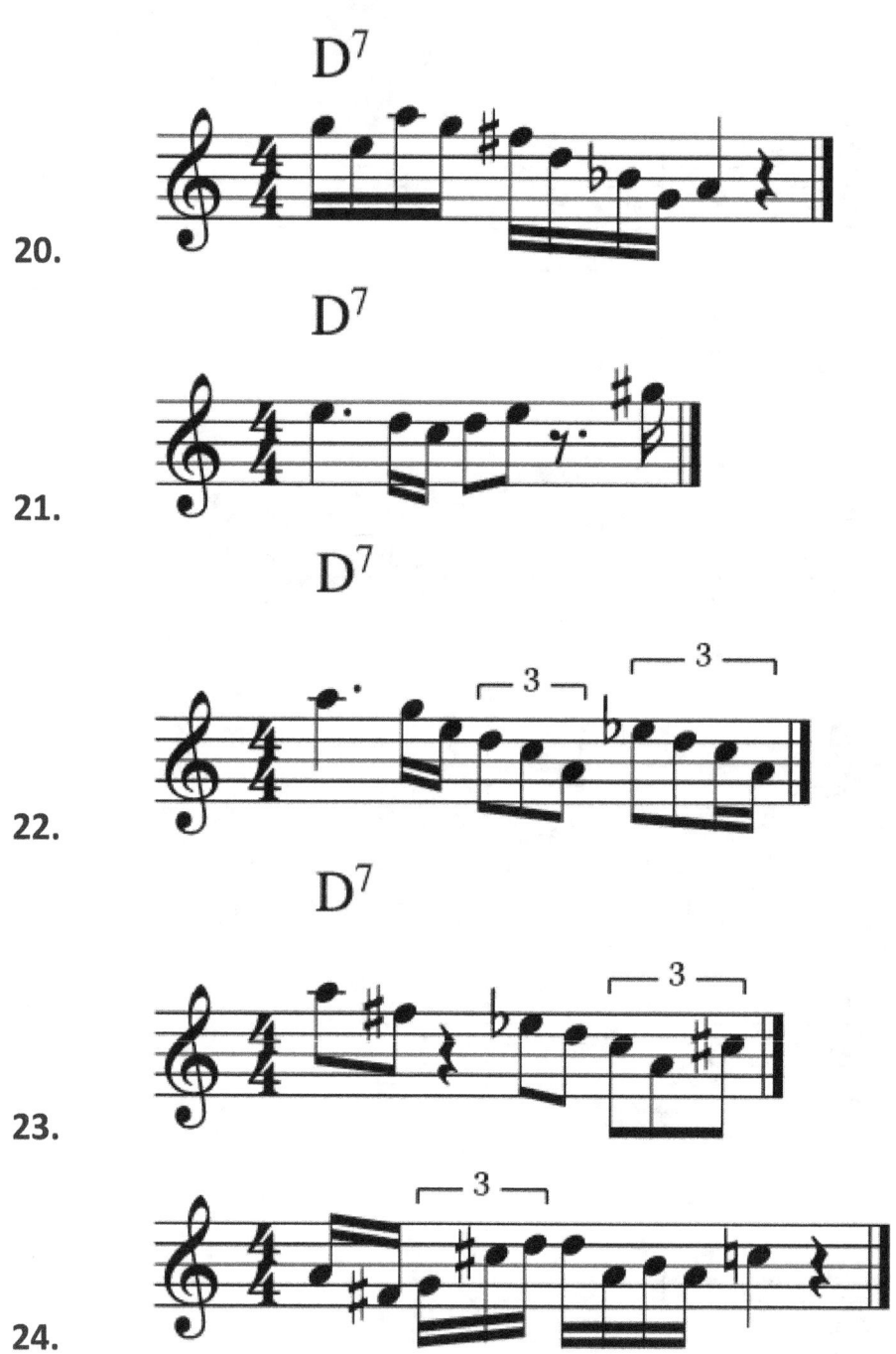

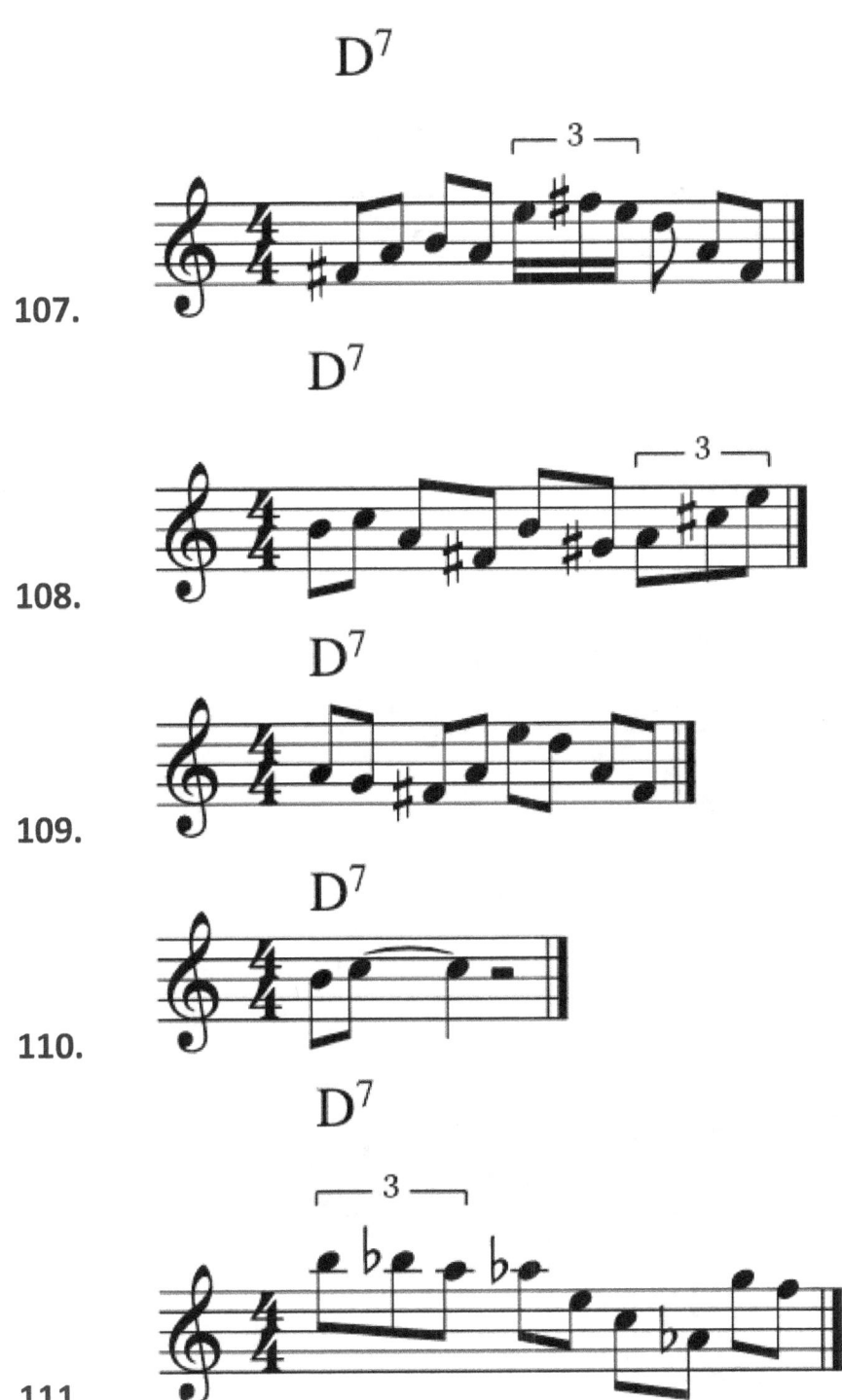

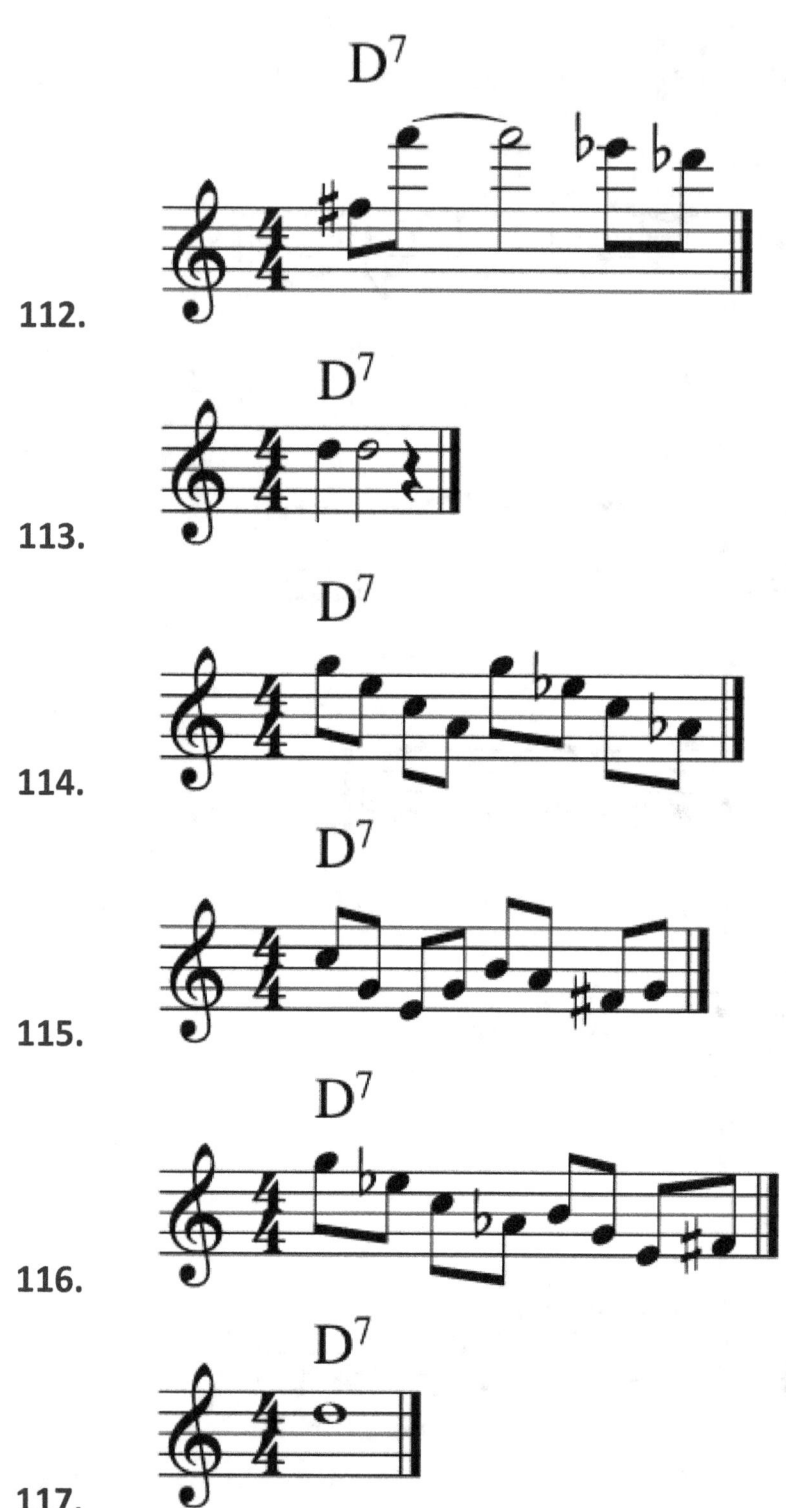

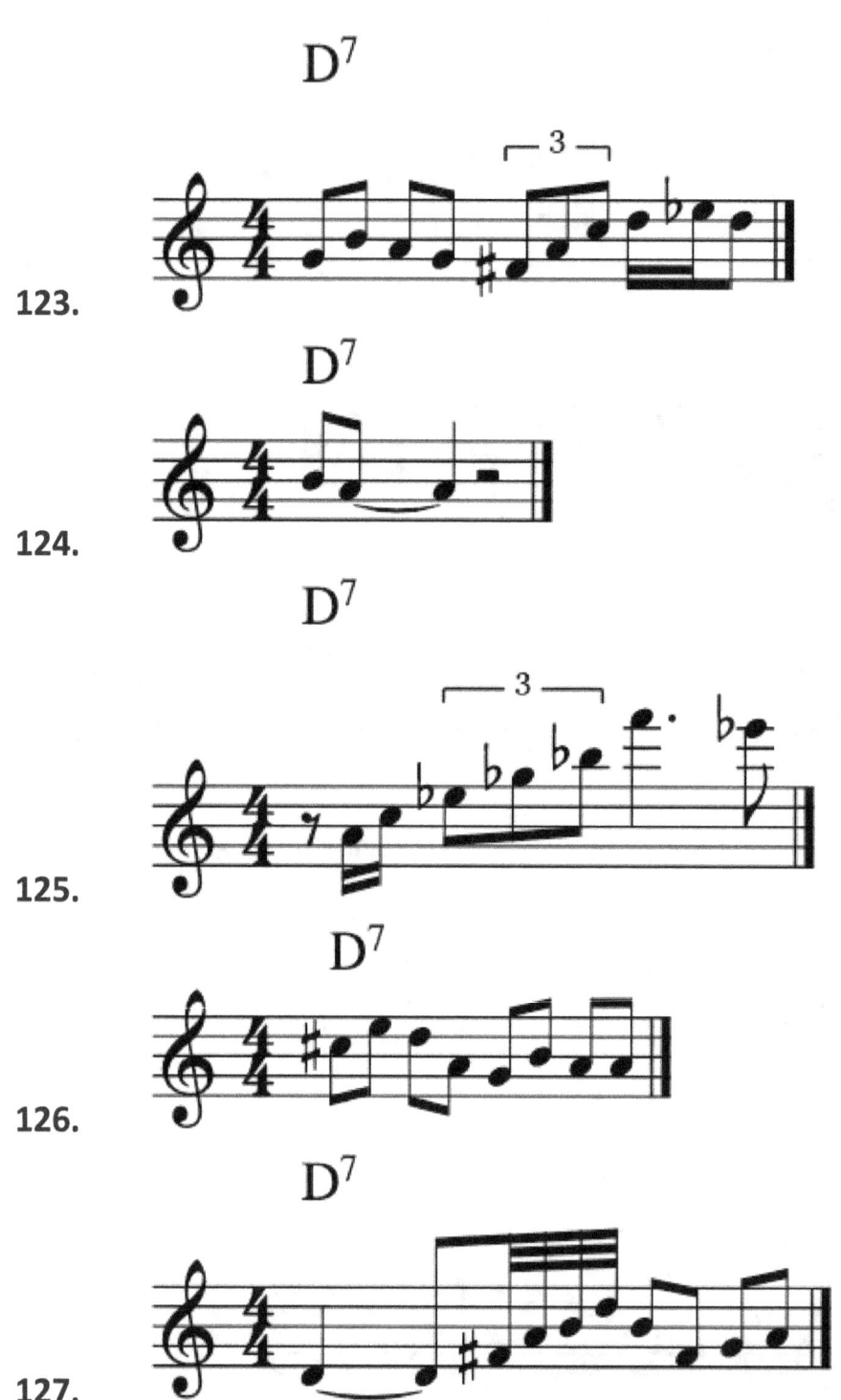

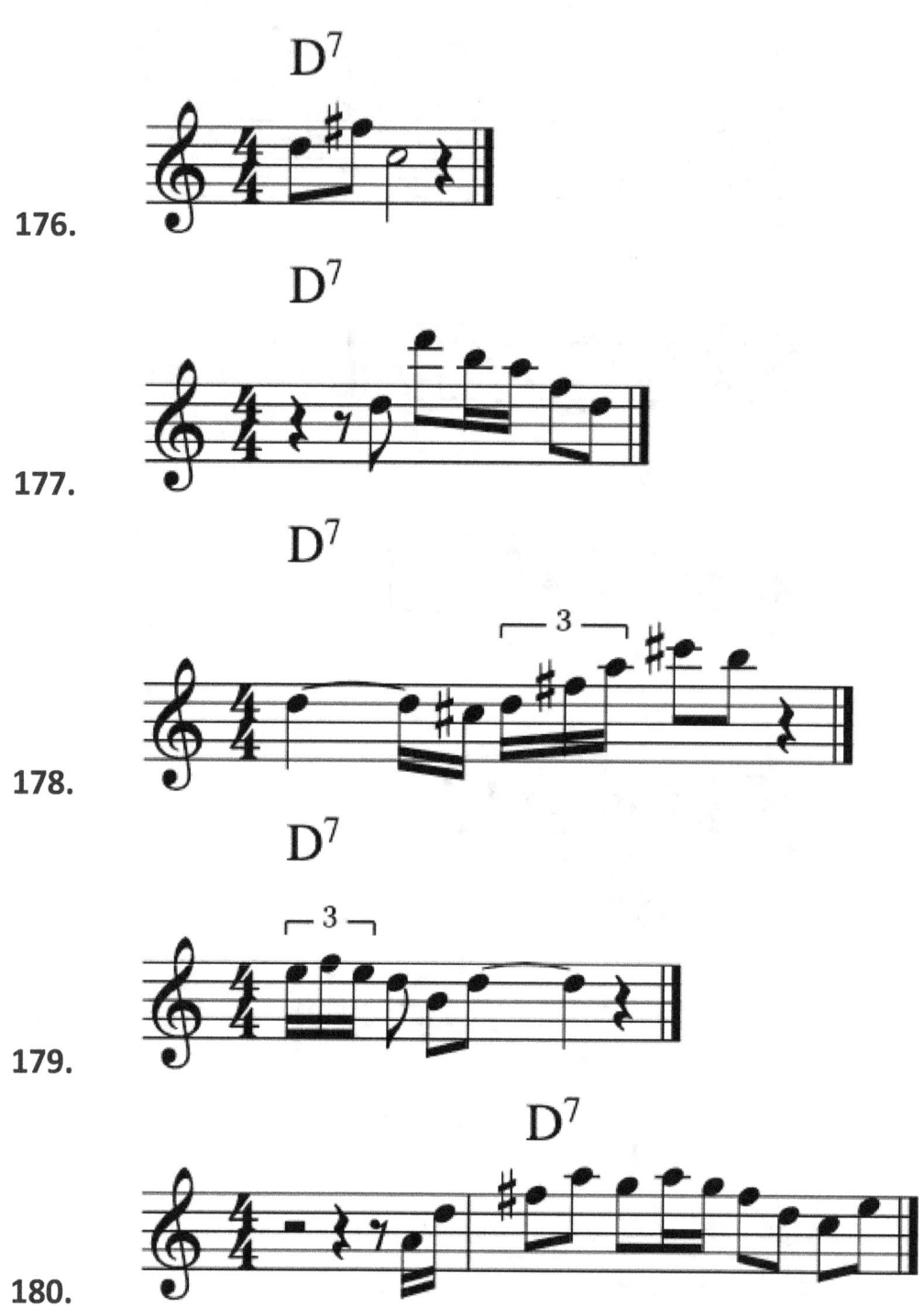

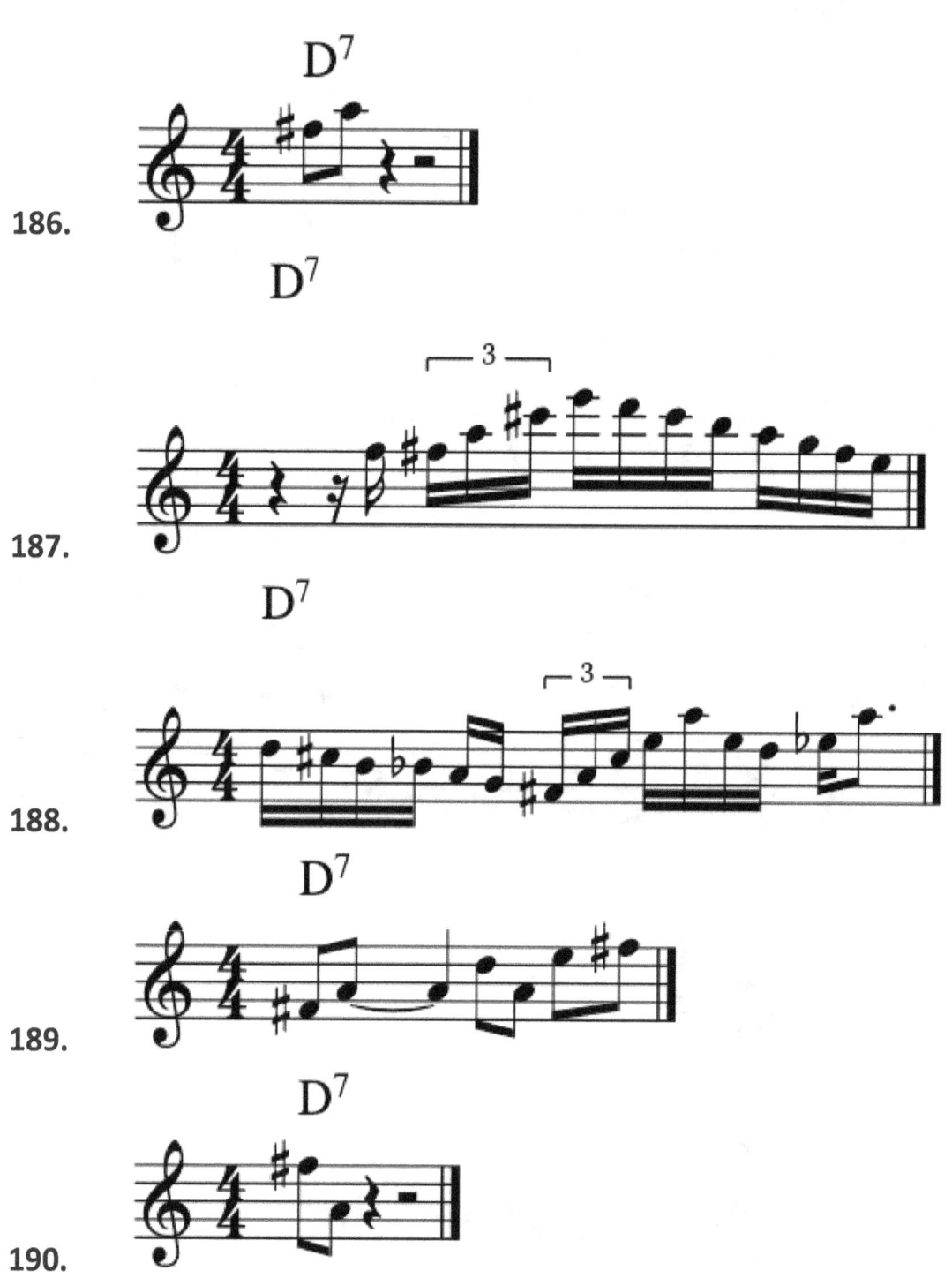

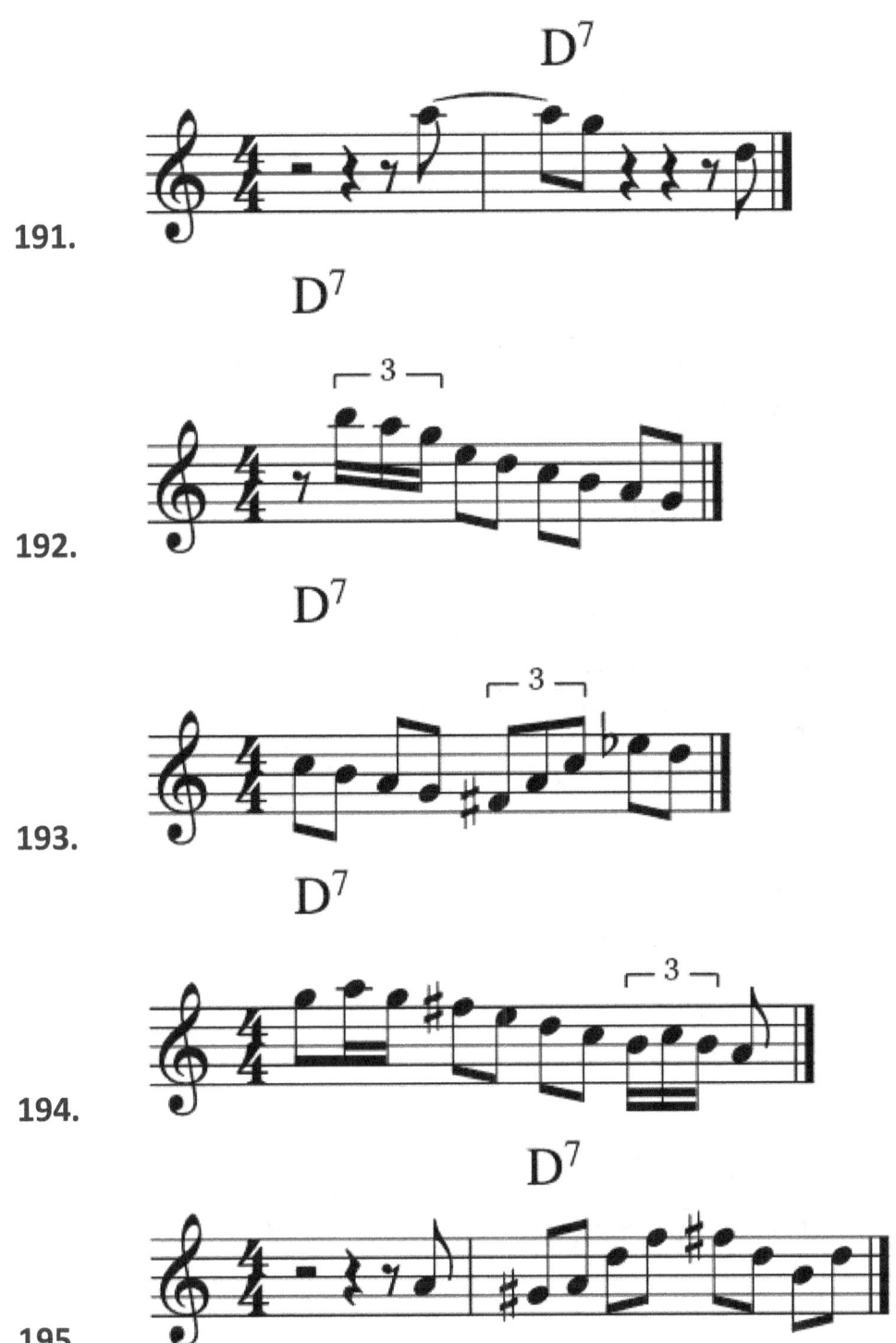

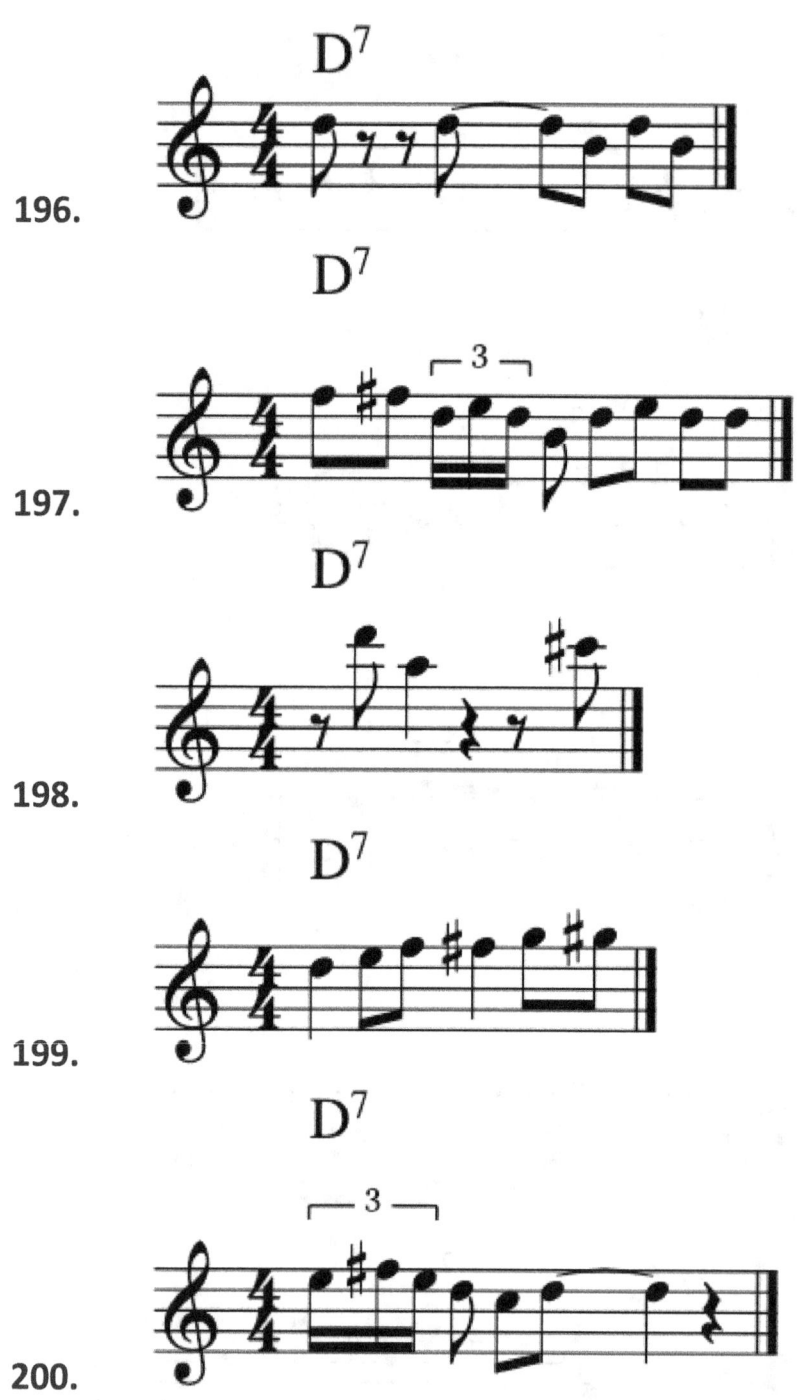

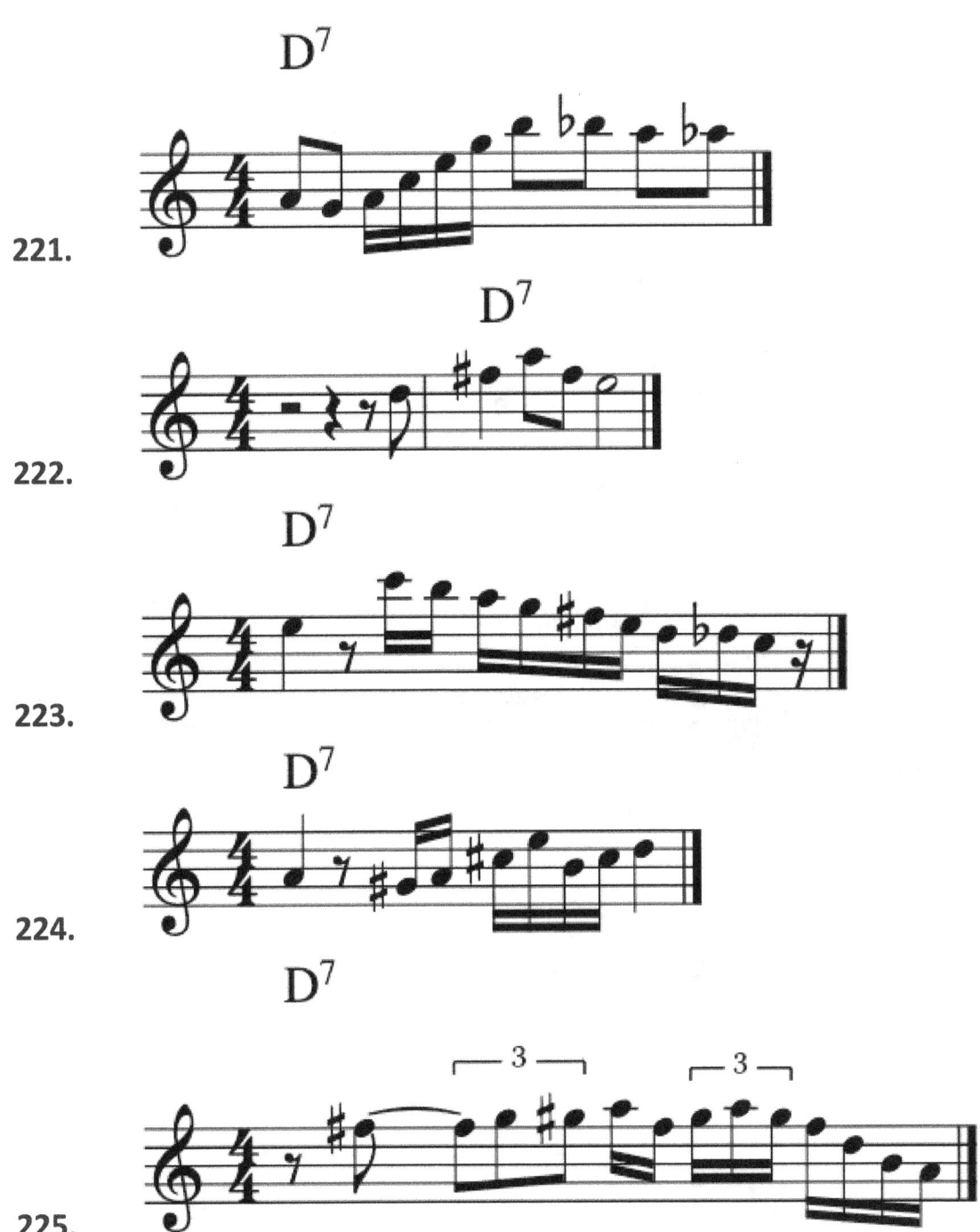

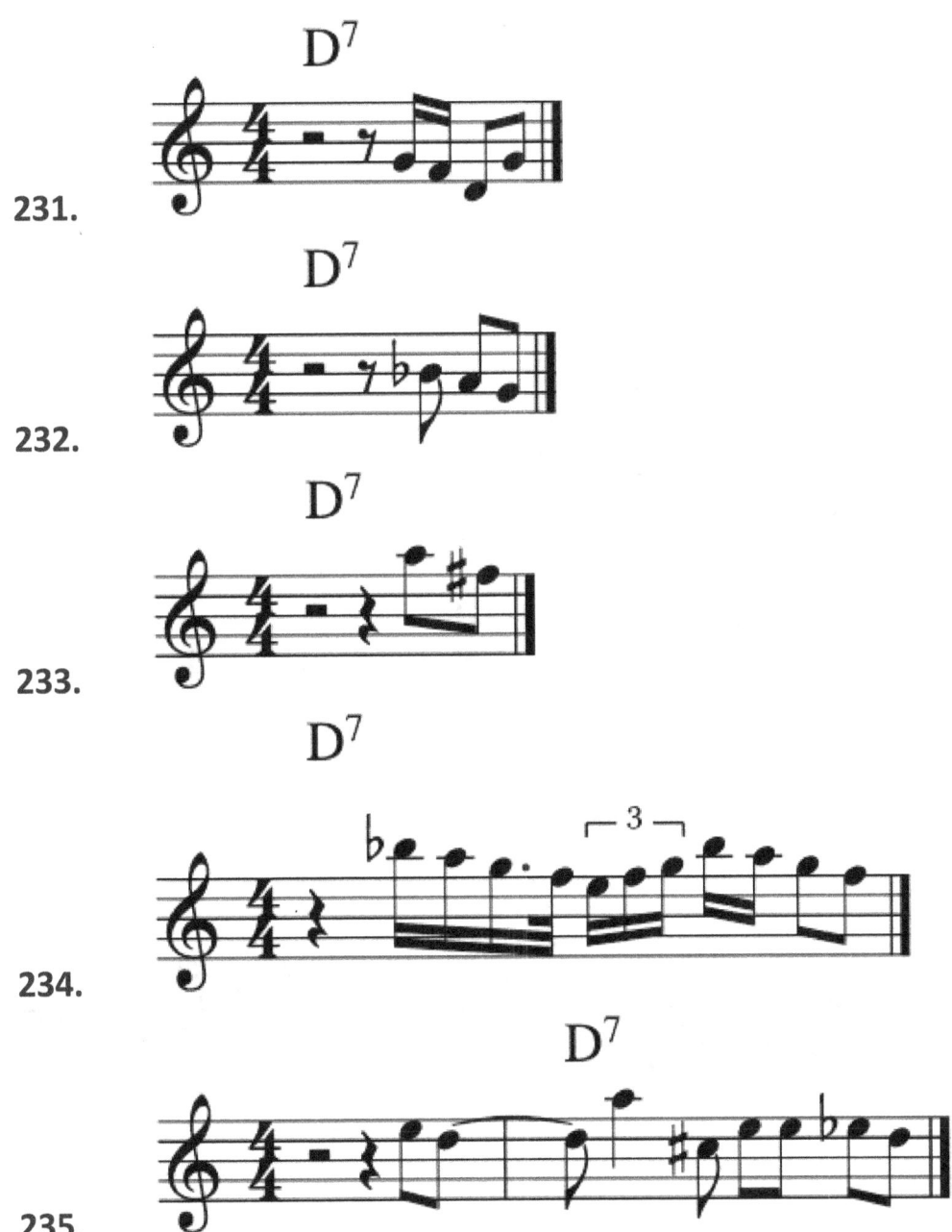

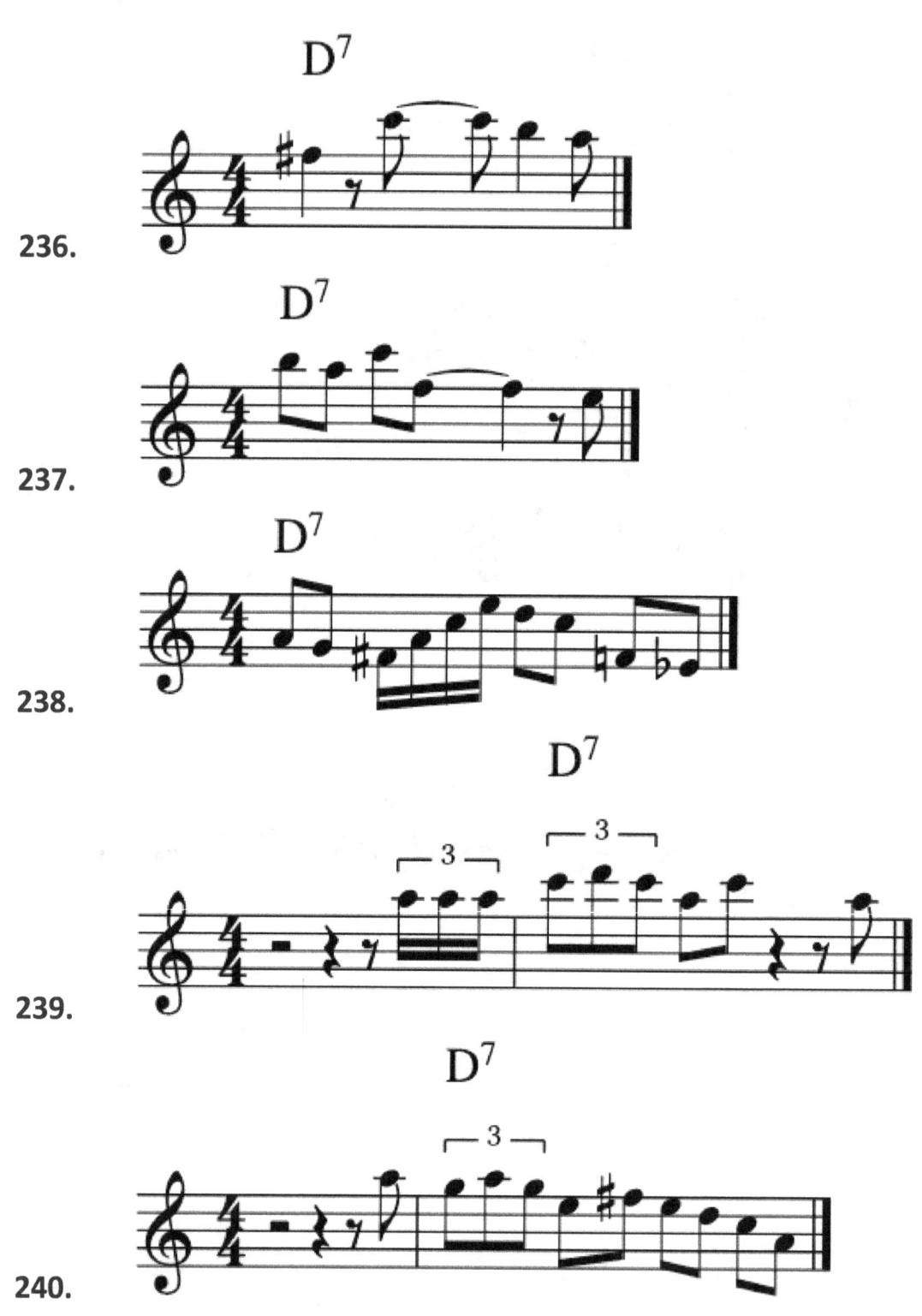

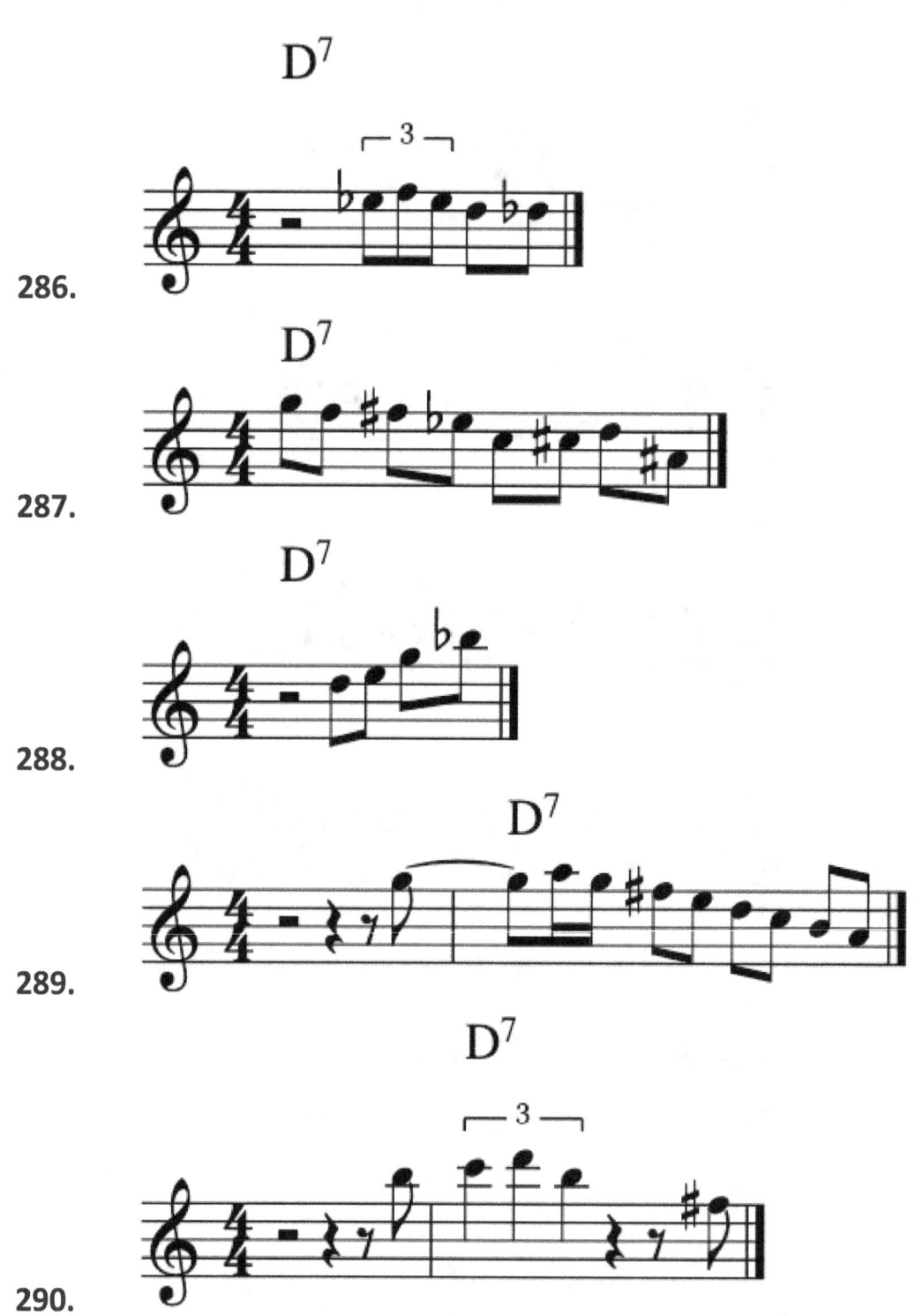

307.

308.

309.

310.

Eb7

E7

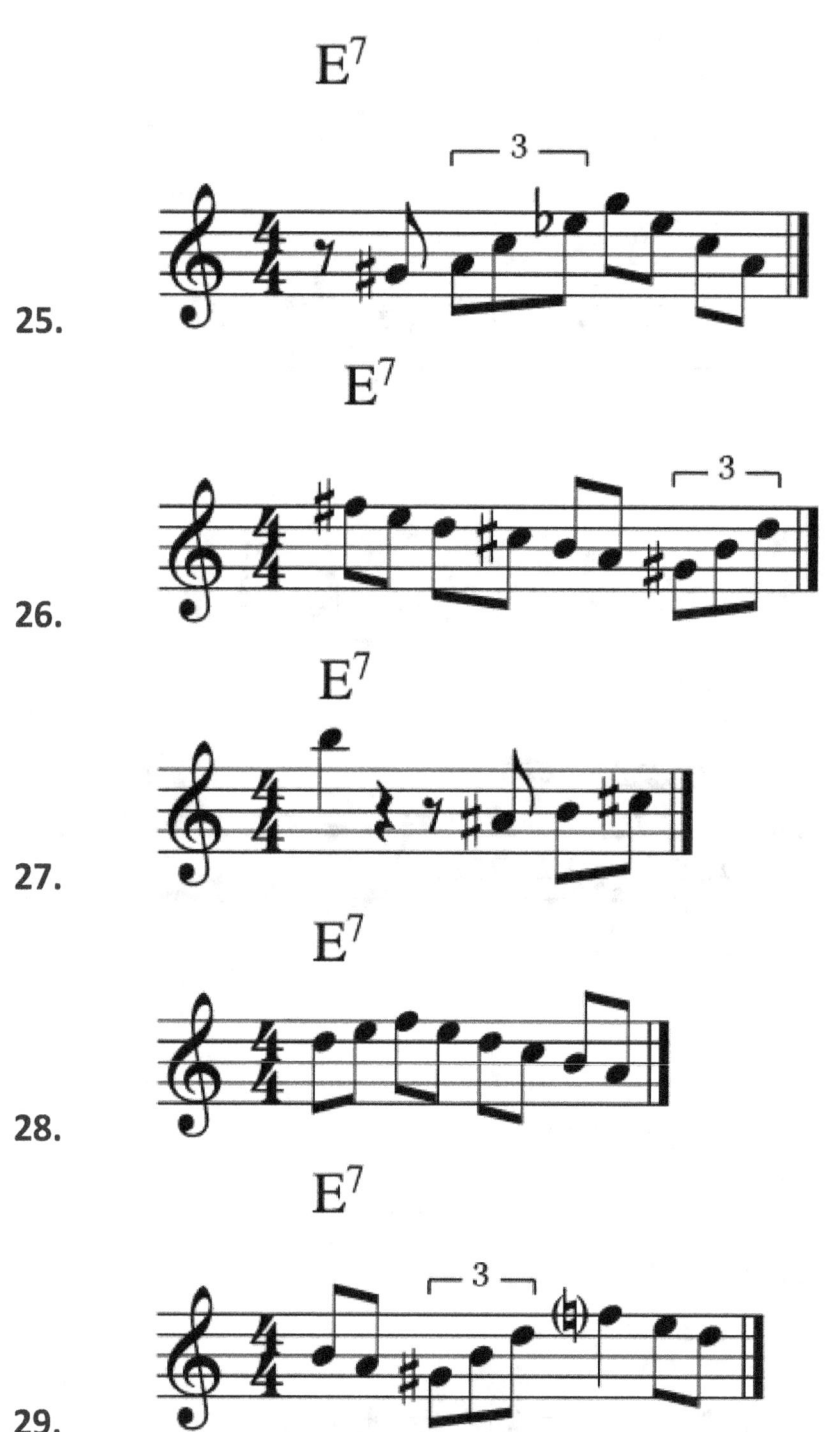

137.

138.

139.

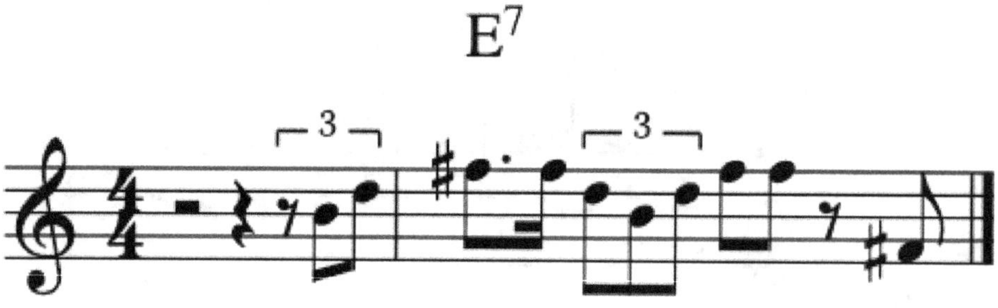

140.

F7

1.

2.

3.

4.

5.

10.

13.

14.

15.

16.

17.

18. F^7

19. F^7

20. F^7

21. F^7

22.

23.

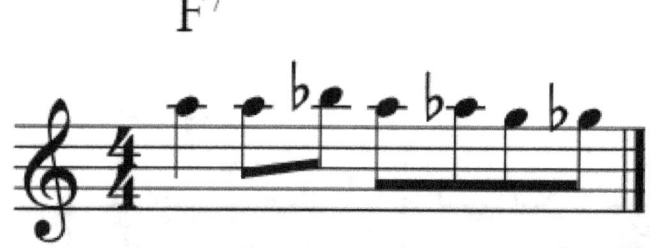

24.

25.

26.

27.

28.

29.

30.

31.

32.

33.

34.

35.

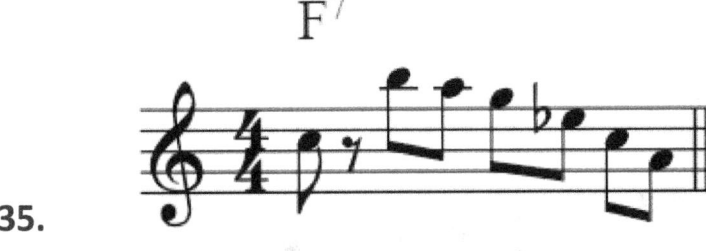

36.

37.

51.

52.

53.

54.

68.

69.

F#7 (Gb7)

1.

2.

25.

G7

1.

2.

3.

31.

32.

33.

34.

35.

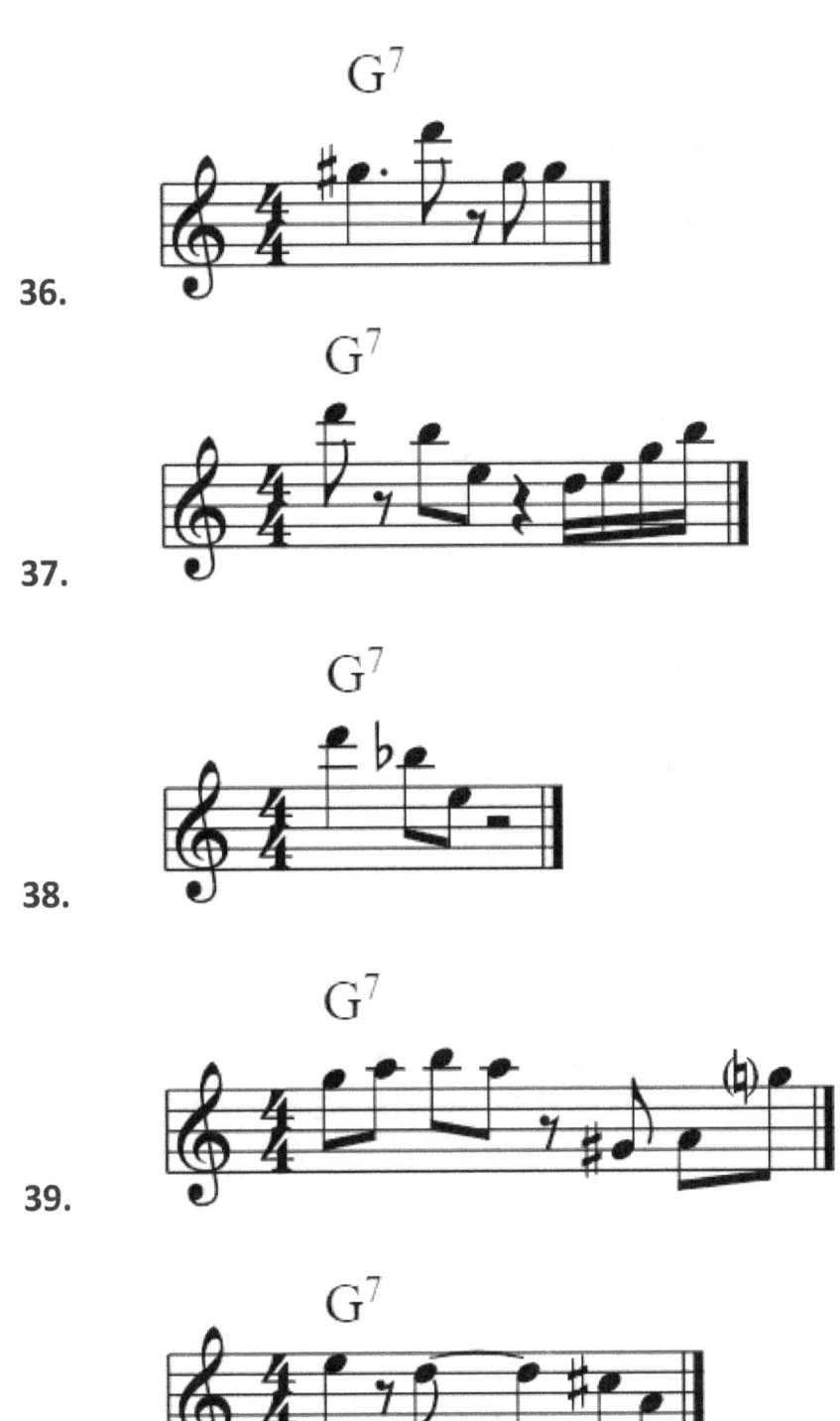

55.

56.

57.

58.

110.

111.

112.

113.

114.

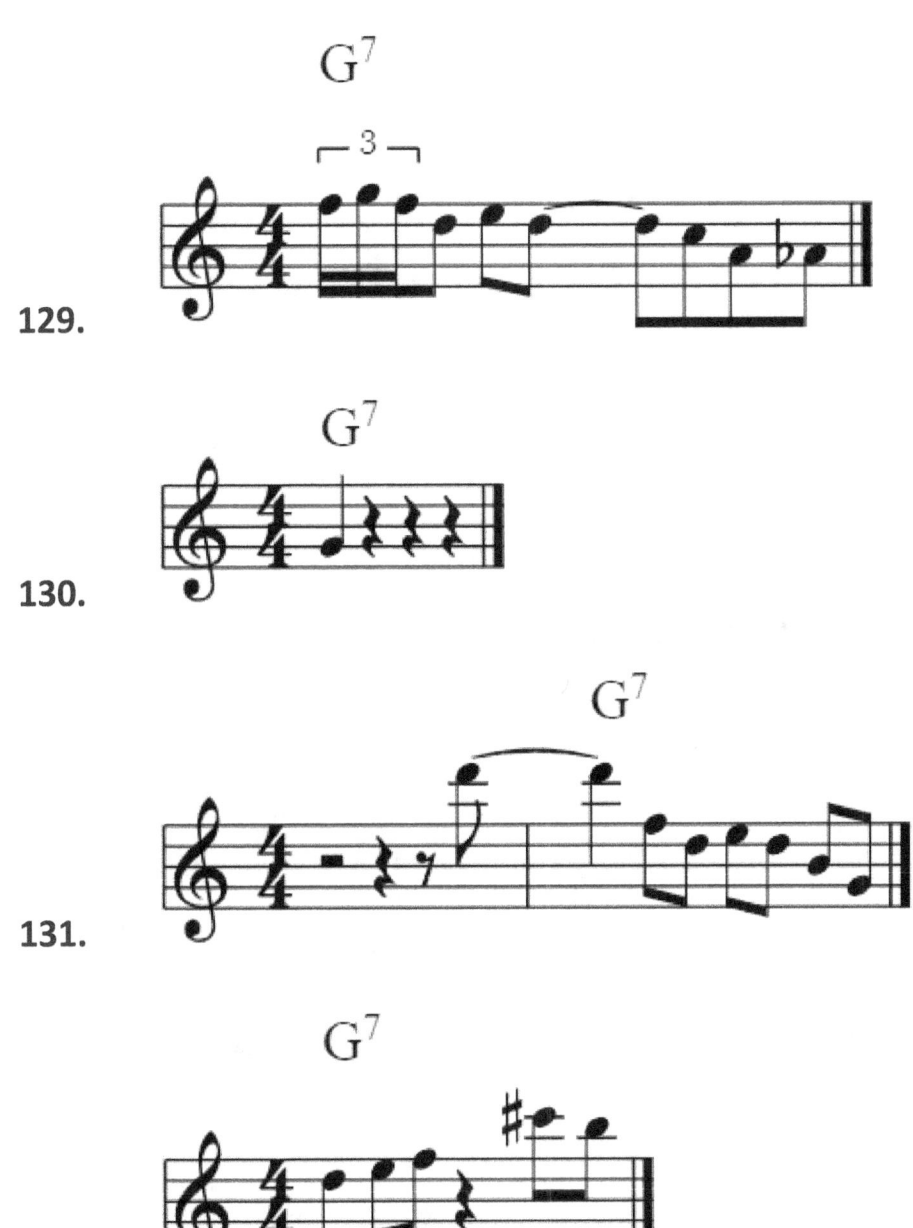

145.

146.

147.

148.

149.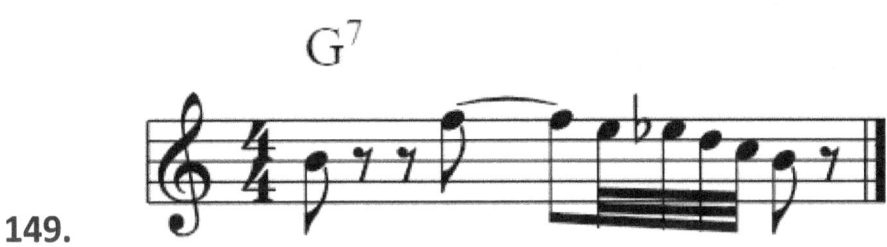

173.

174.

175.

176.

181.

182.

183.

184.
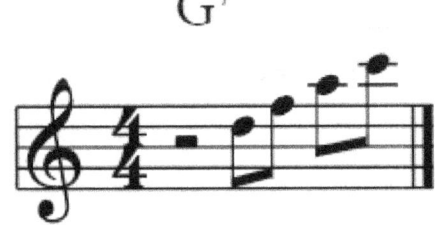

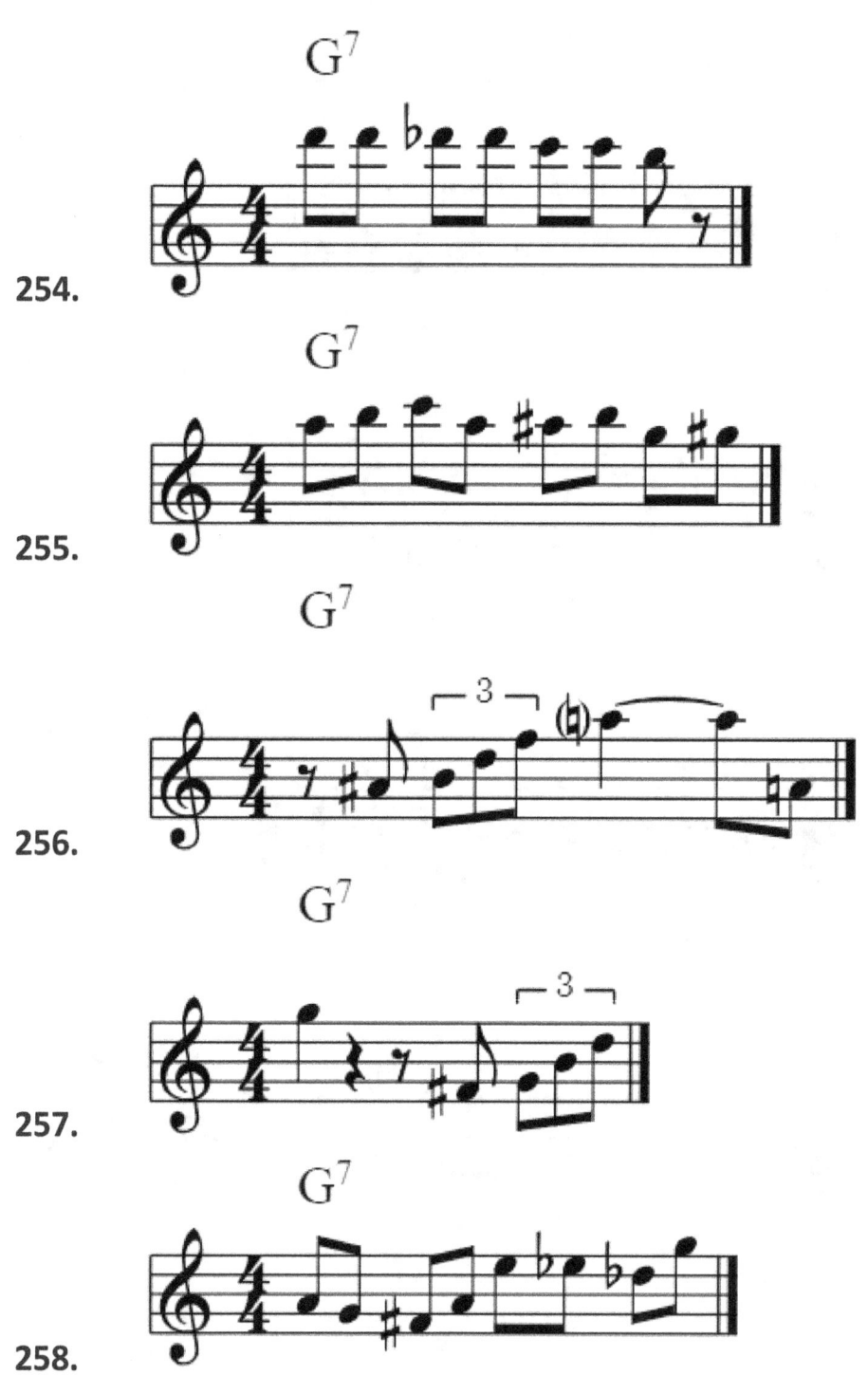

314.

Dominant 7b9 Chords:

A7b9

1.

2.

3.

D7b9

E7 b9

F#7b9

2.

Dominant 7+9 Chords:

Ab7+9

1.

B7+9

1.

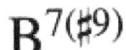

E7+9

Dominant 7b9+9 Chords:

D7b9+9

1.

Dominant 7 #11:

G7 #11

1.

2.

3.

Dominant 7 Progressions:

Dominant 7 to Major:

C7 to Ab

1.

2.

3.

4.

Dominant 7 to Dominant 7:

A7 to E7

1.

A7 to F#7

1.

2.

A7 to G7

3.

4.

C7 to A7

1.
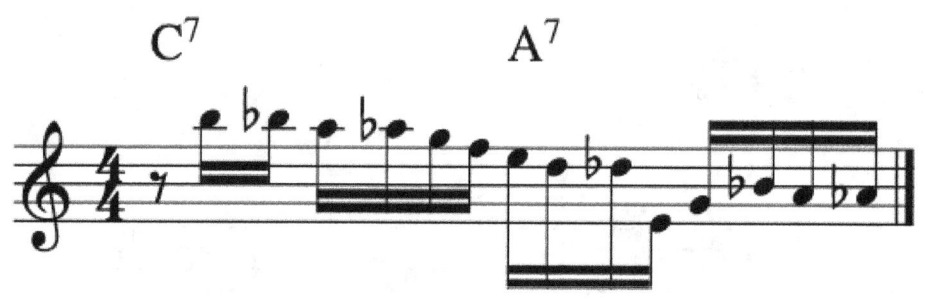

C7 to Bb7

C7 to C#7

1.

C7 to G7

1.

Db7 to D7

1.

D7 to A7

1.

D7 to B7

1.

2.

3.

D7 to G7

1.

Eb7 to E7

1.

E7 to A7

1.

G7 to D7

1.

G7 to E7

Dominant 7 to Dominant 7b9:

A7 to F#7b9

E7 to E7b9

1.

G7 to E7b9

1.

Dominant 7 to Minor:

C7 to C min

D7 to D min

1.

2.

G7 to A min

1.

G7 to Bb min

1.

Dominant 7 to Half Diminished 7:

C7 to C#ø7

1.

Dominant 7 to Fully Diminished:
C7 to C# 0

D7 to F#0 (Gb0)

3.

G7 to G0

1.

G7 to G#0 (Ab0)

1.

Dominant 7 to Augmented 7:

C7 to C+7

1.

2.

Dominant 7 to Major to Fully Diminished:

G7 to C to C#0

Dominant 7 to Dominant 7 to Fully Diminished:

G7 to C7 to C#0

Dominant 7 to Minor to Dominant 7:

G7 to Bb min to Eb7

1.

G7 to D min to G7

1.

Dominant 7 Slash Chords:
G7/D to D7

1.

Chapter #3

Minor Chords and Progressions

Minor Chords:

Ab minor

4.

5.

6.

A minor

1.

Am

2.

Am

3.

Am

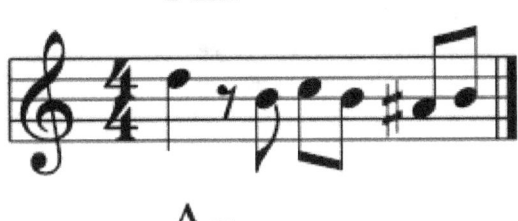

4.

Am

5.

Am

6.

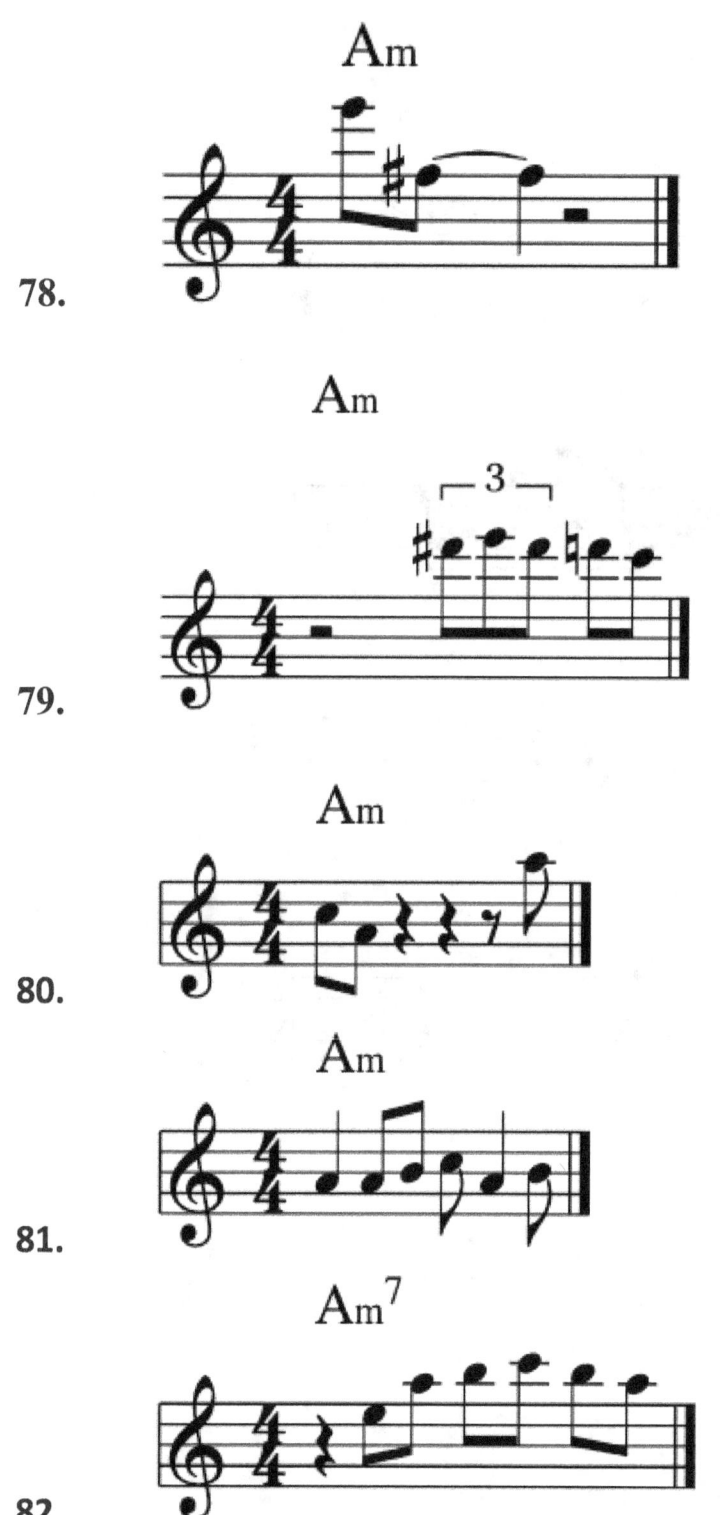

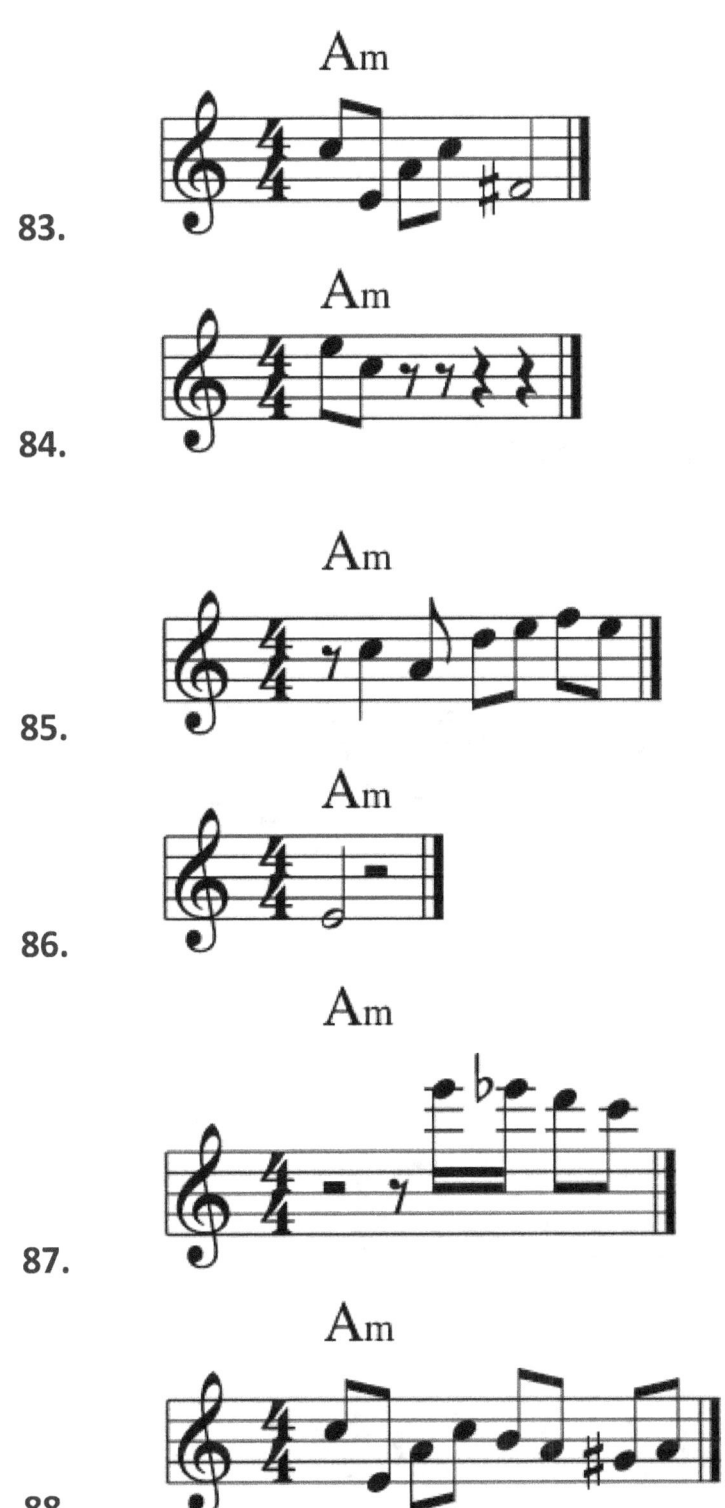

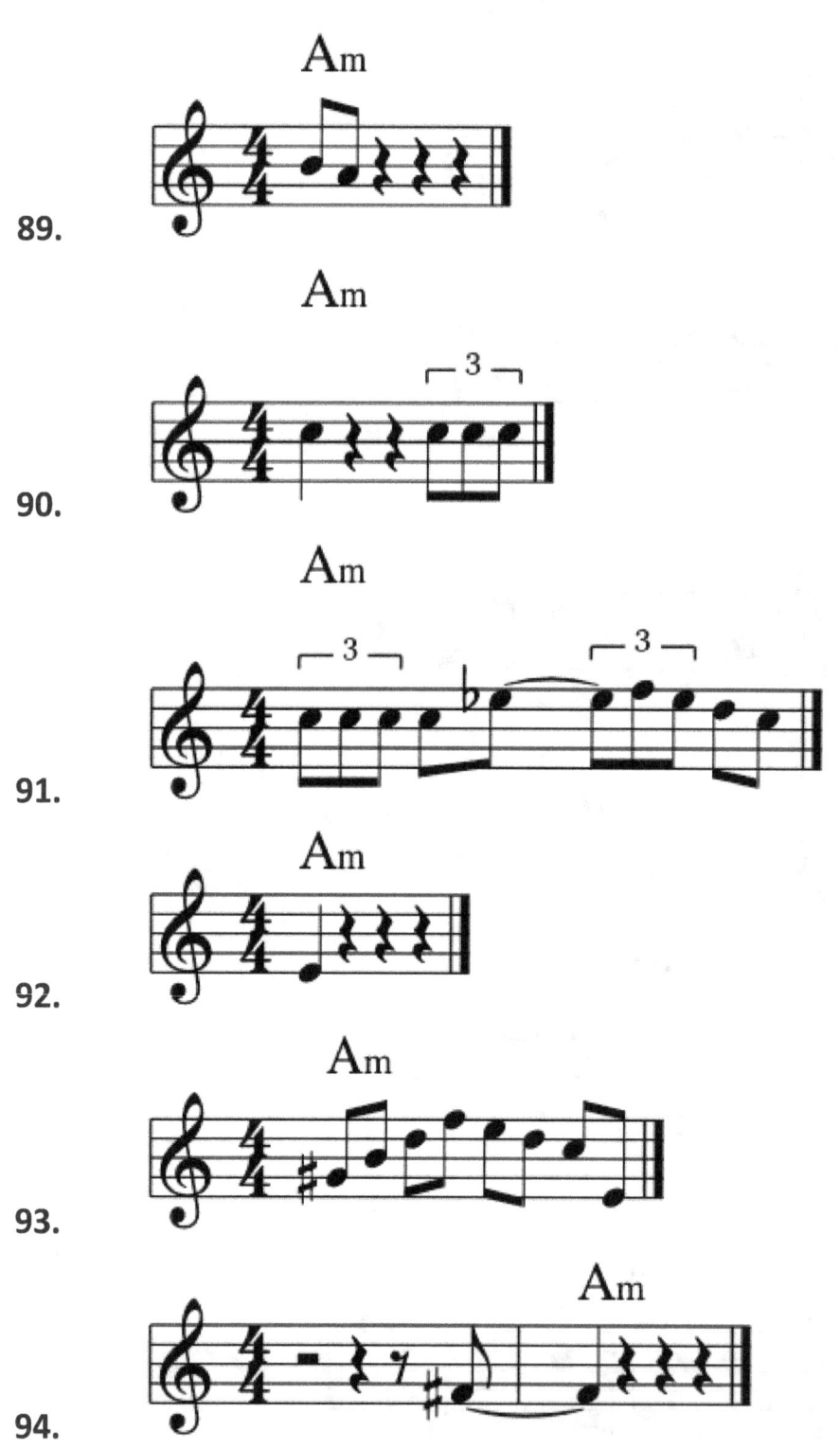

115.

Am

116.

Am

117.

Am

118.

Am

Bb minor

B minor

C minor

C# minor

D minor

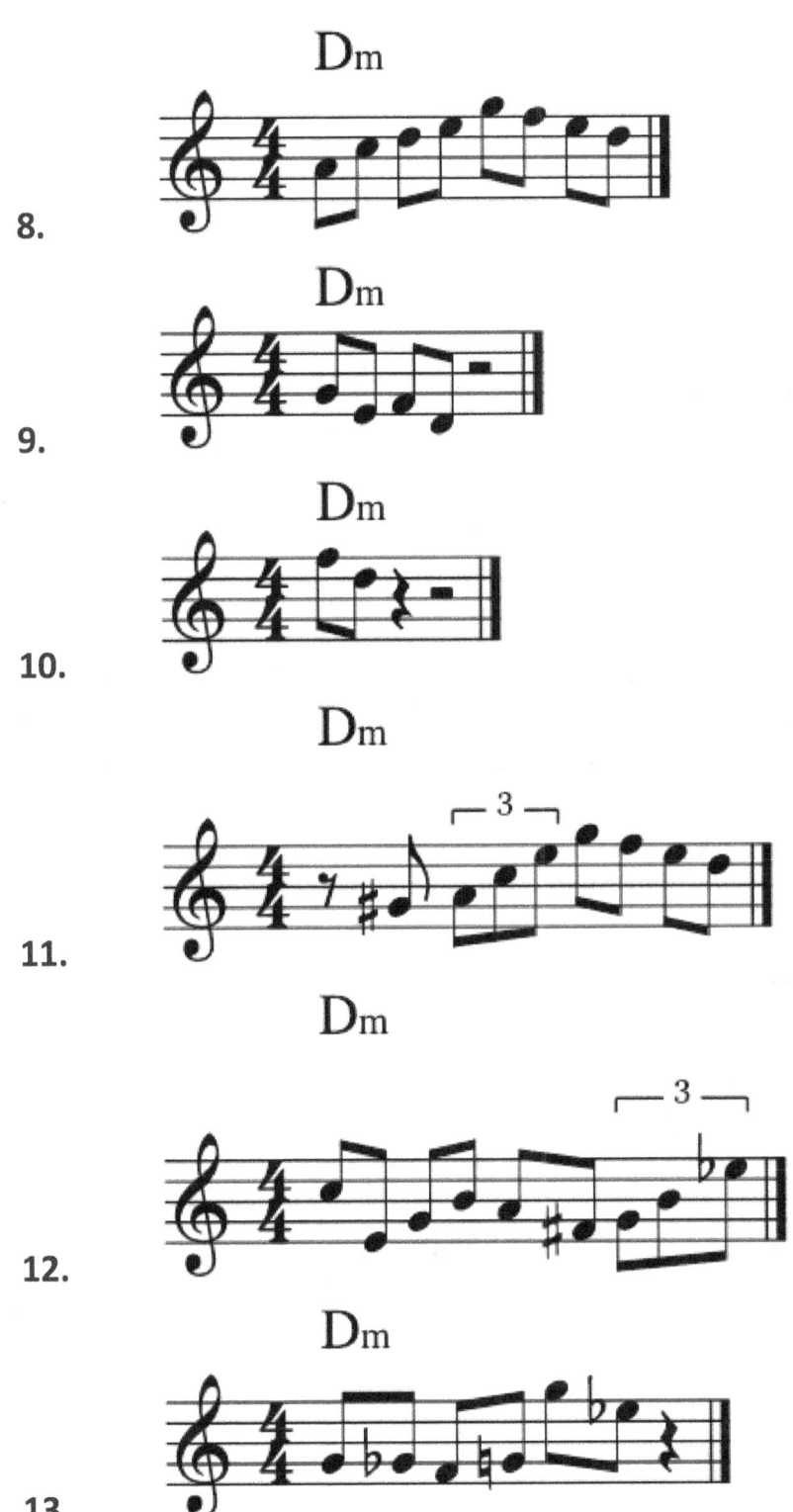

55.

E minor

1.

2.

3.

4.

44.

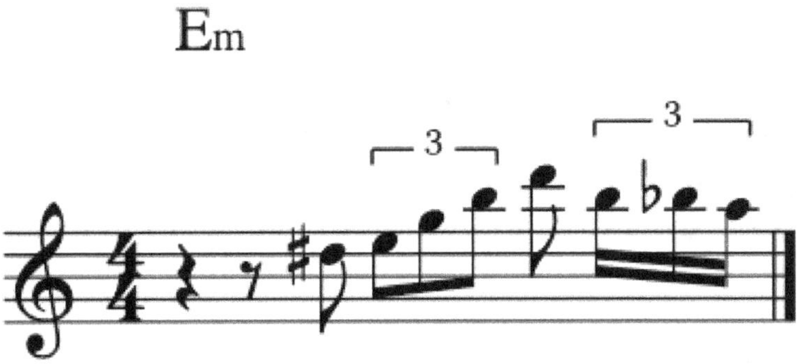

45.

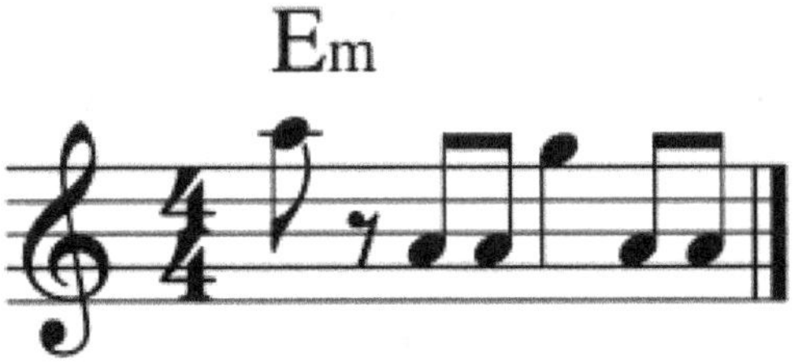

46.

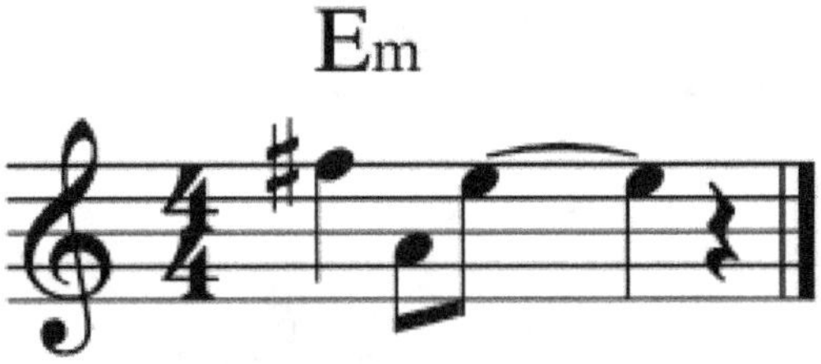

47.

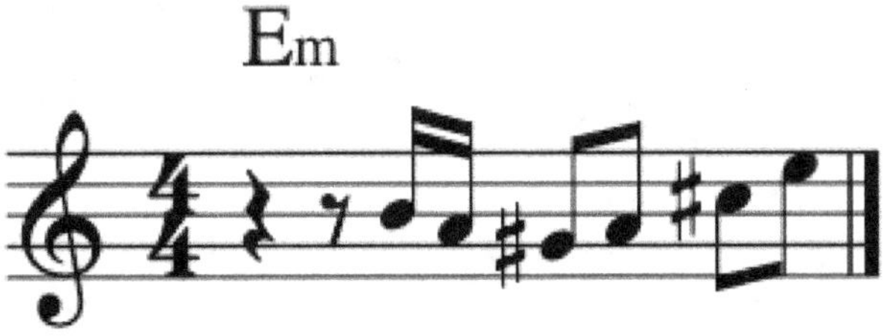

48.

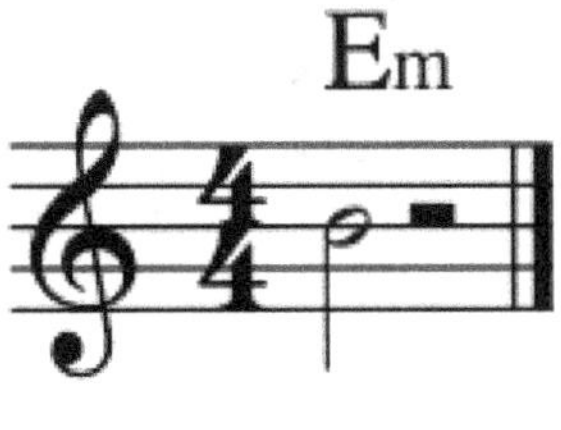

49.

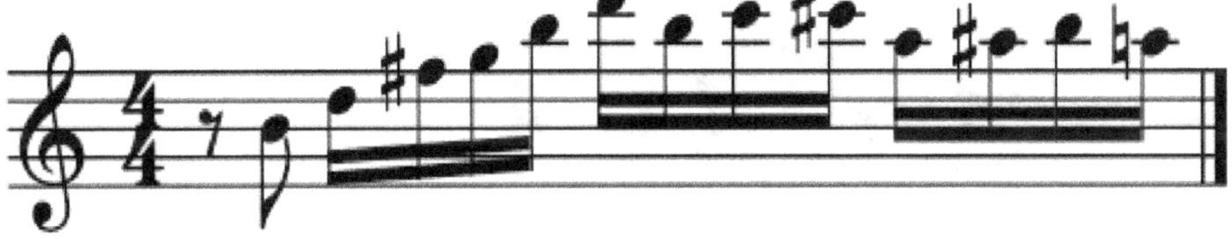

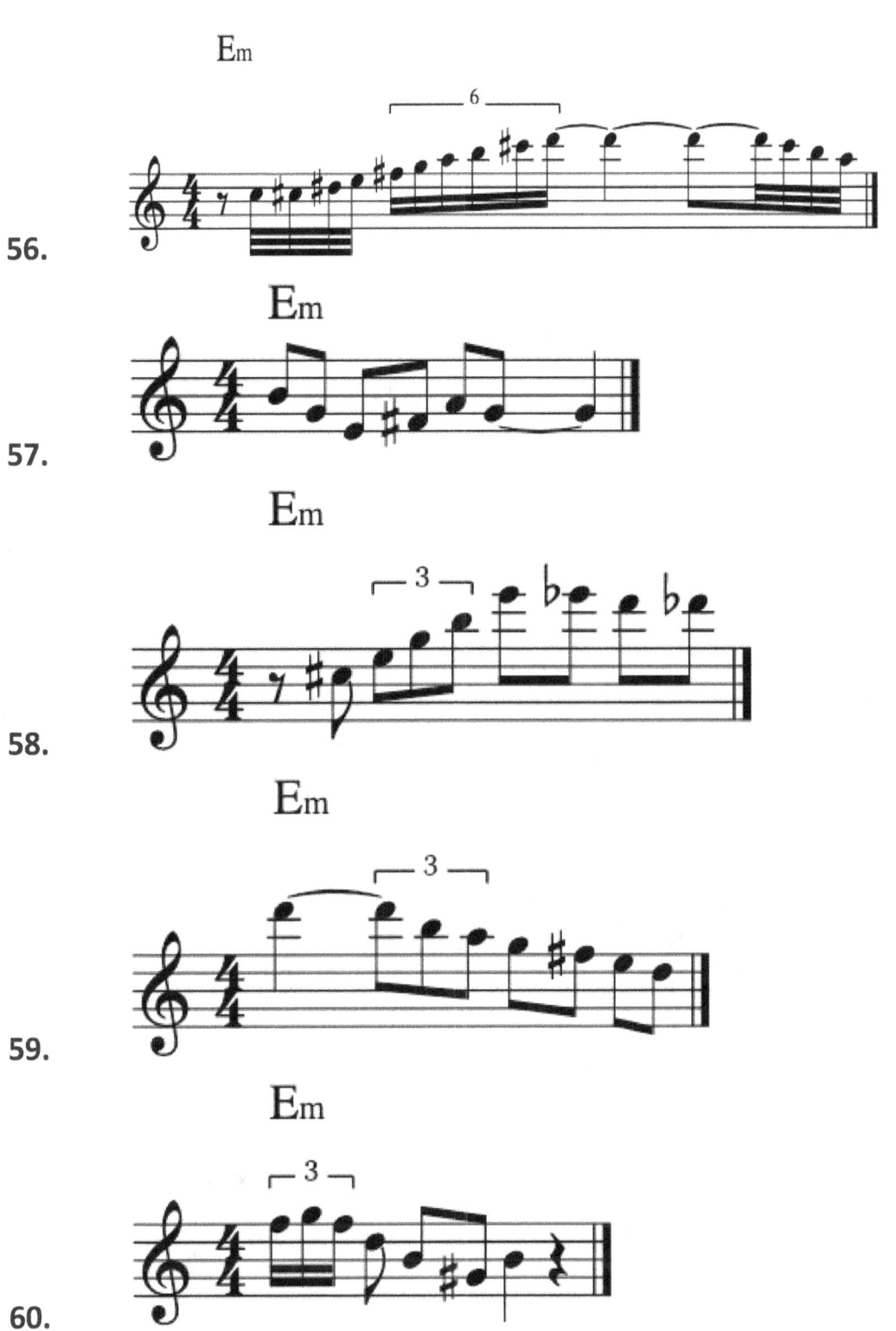

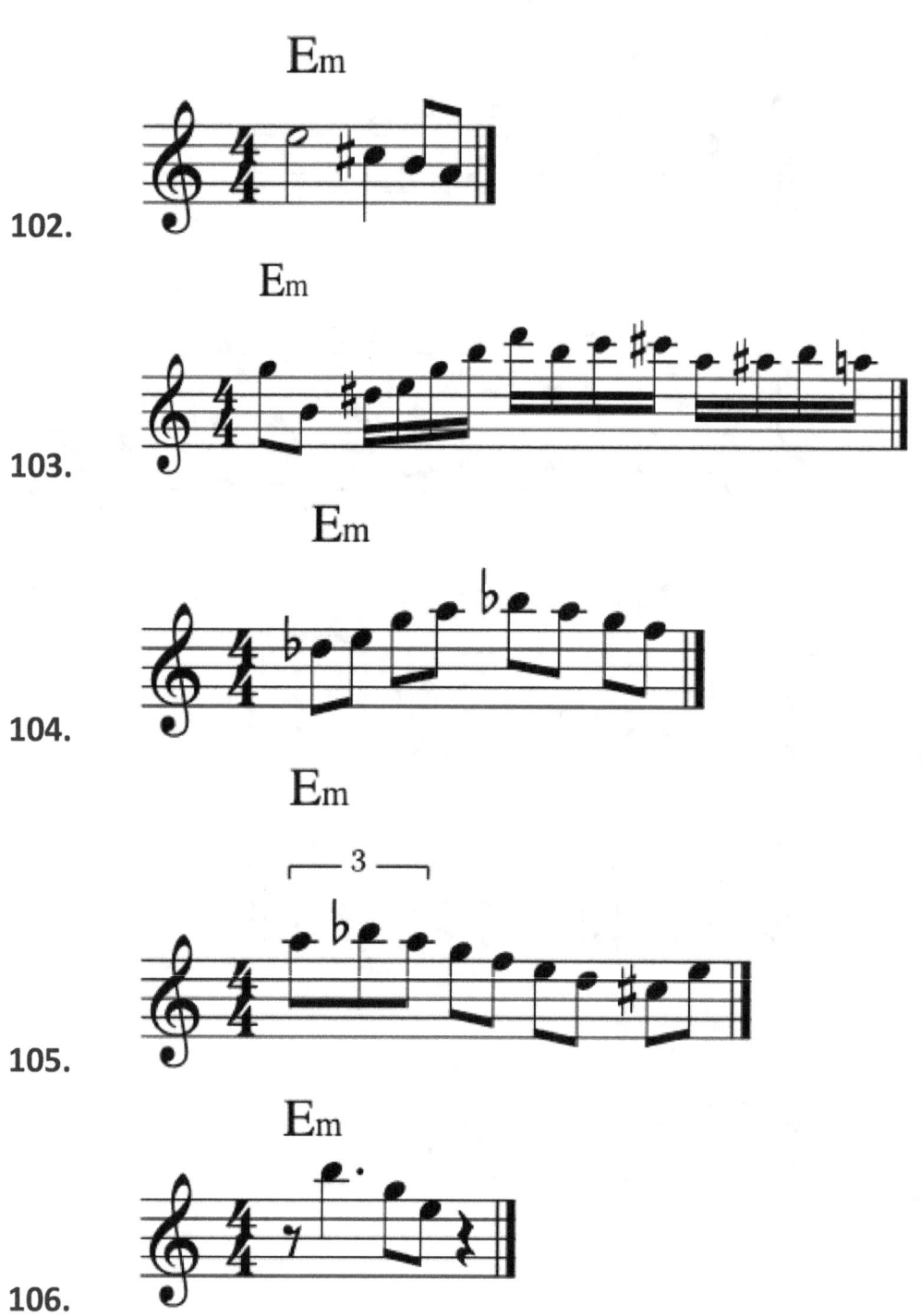

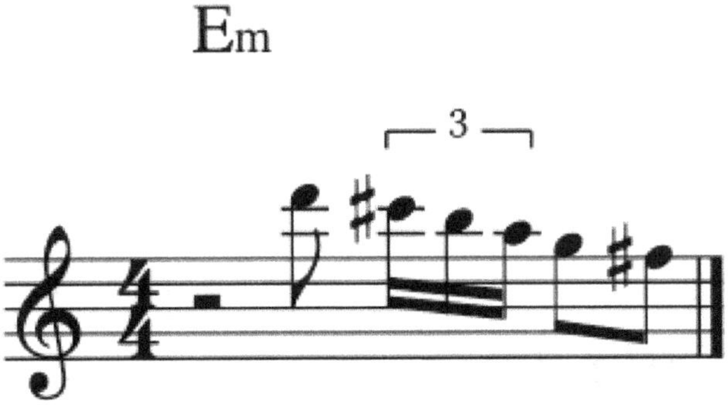

107.

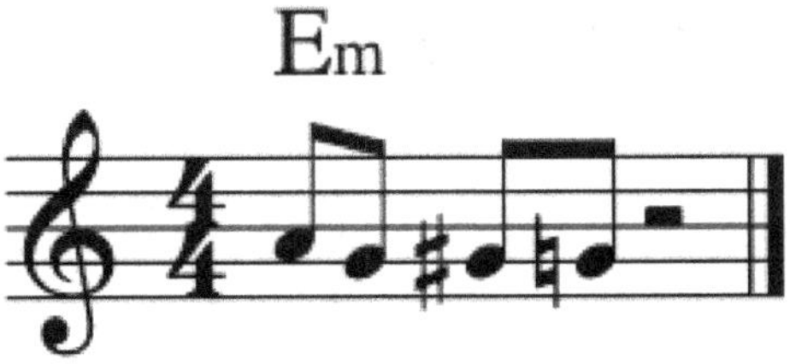

108.

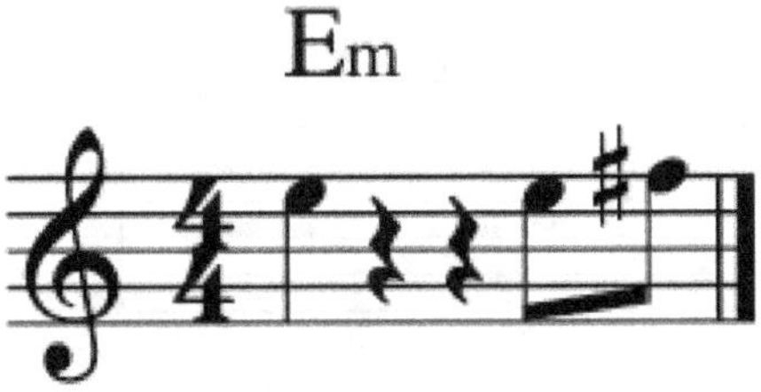

109.

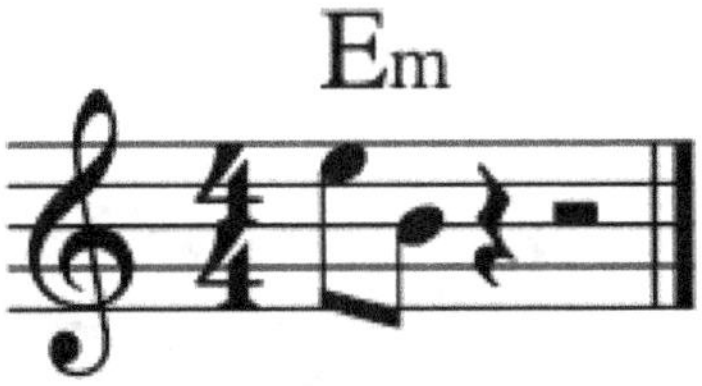

110.

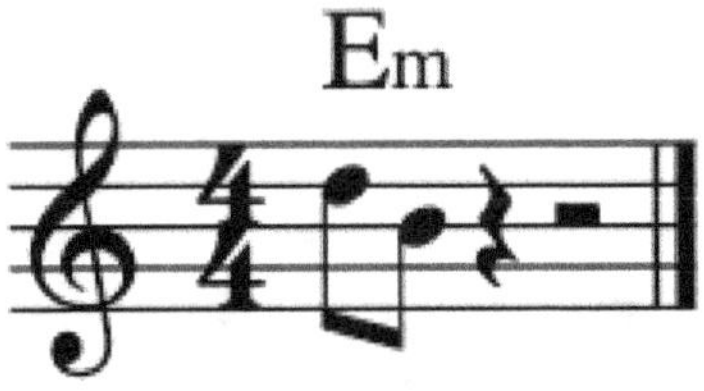

111.

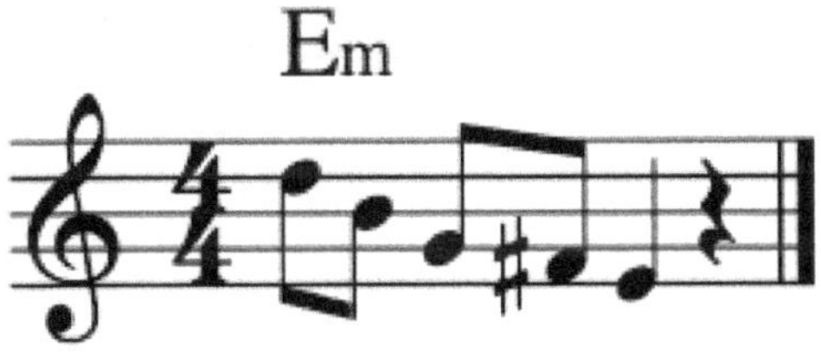

112.

F minor

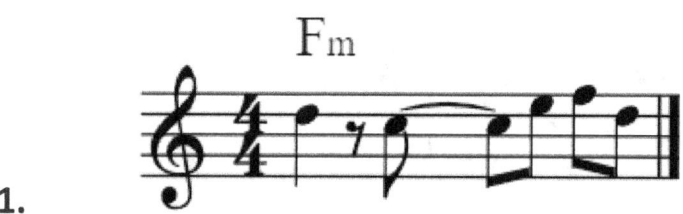

2.

3.

4.

5.

6.

F# minor

1.

2.

3.

8.

9.

10.
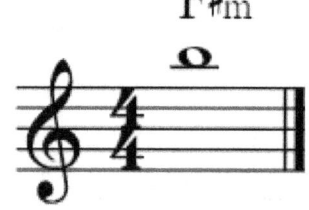

11.

12.

13.

14.

G minor

1.

2.

3.

4.

5.

6.

7.

8.

9.

10.
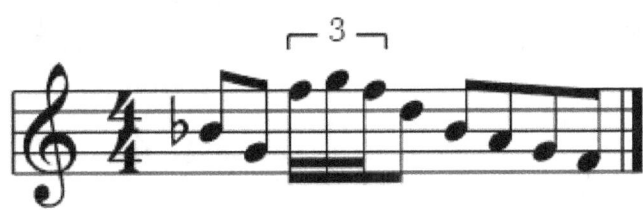

11.

12.

13.

14.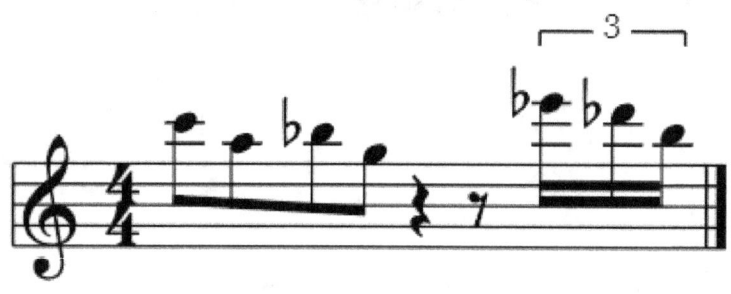

15.

16.

17.

18.

19.

20.

21.

22.

23.

24.

25.

26.

27.

28.

29.

30.

31.

32.

33.

34.

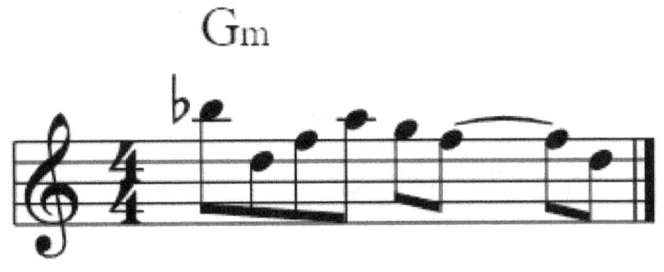

35.

36.

37.

42.

43.

44.

45.

46.

47.

48.

49.

50.

51.

52.

53.

54.

55.

56.

57.

58.

59.

60.

61.

62.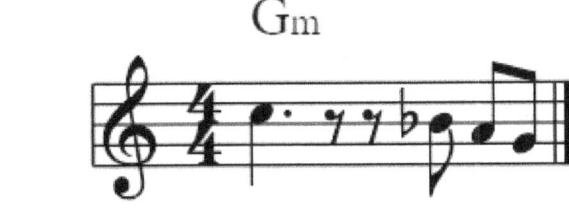

63.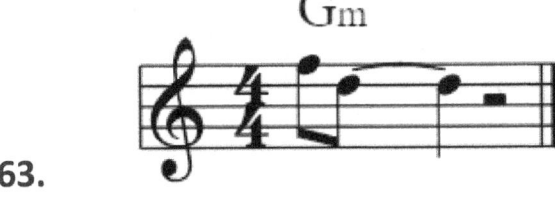

69.

70.

G# minor

1.

2.

Minor Progressions:

Minor to Major:

A min to Ab

1.

E min to Eb

1.

Minor to Dominant 7:

A min to D7

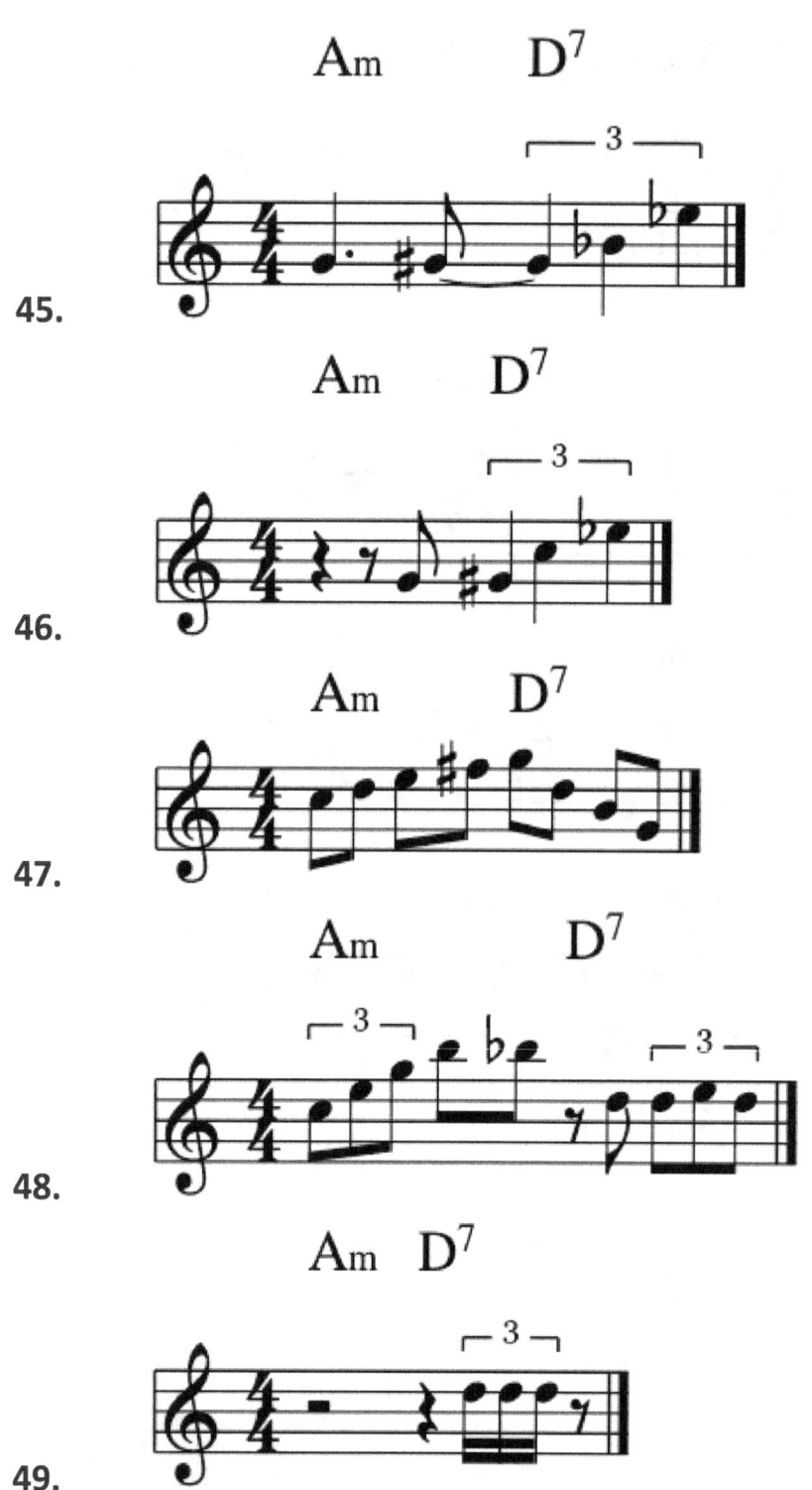

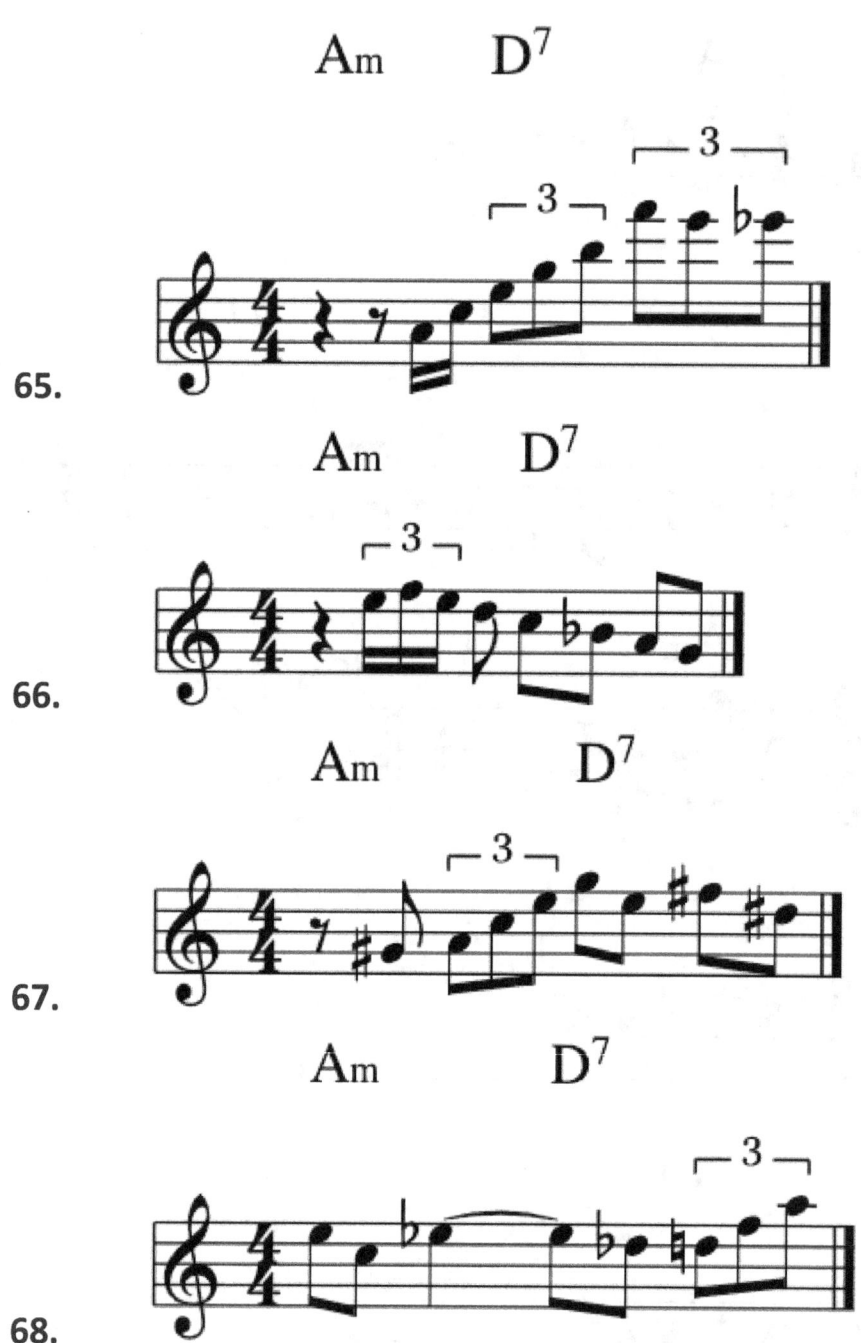

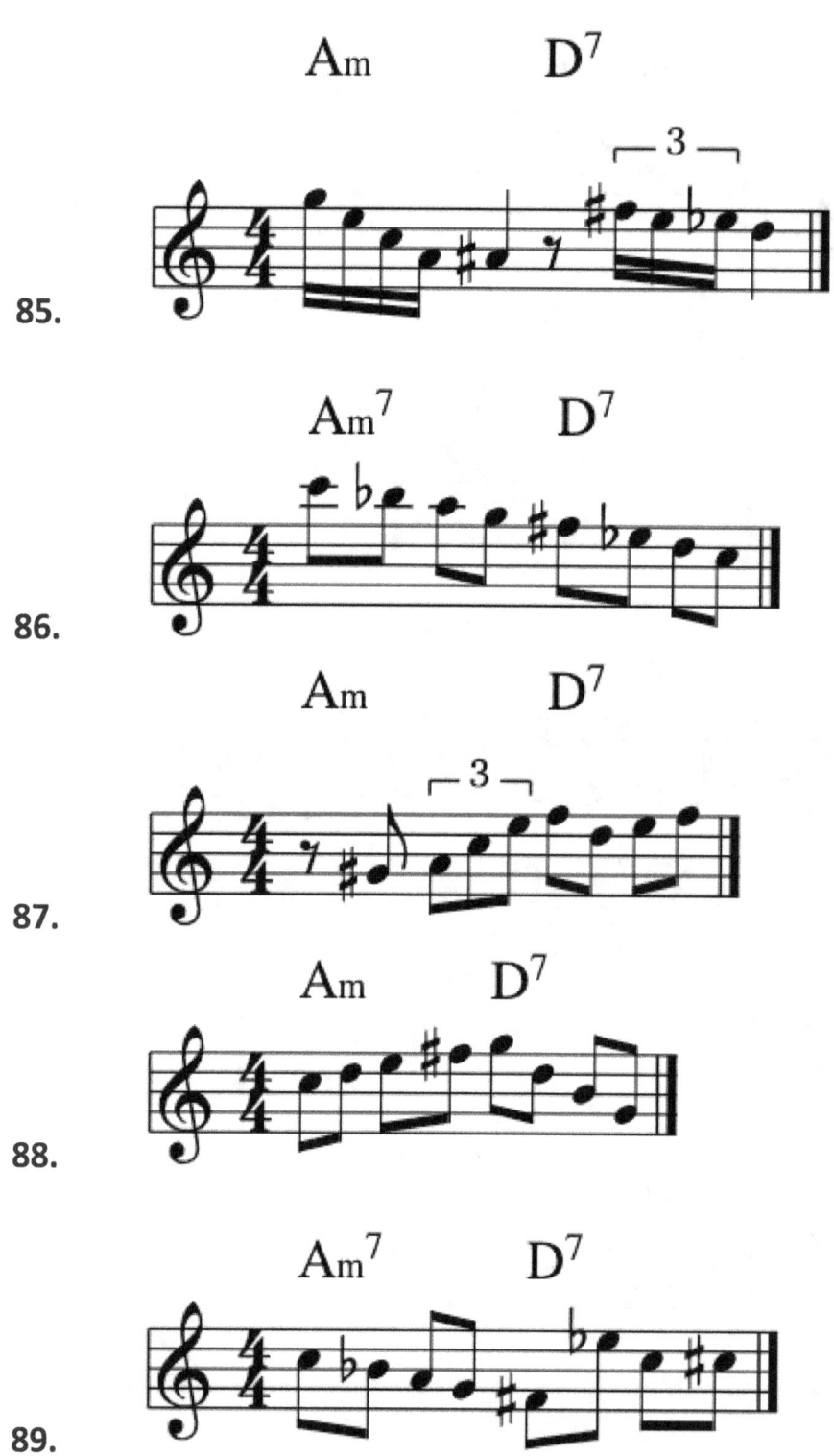

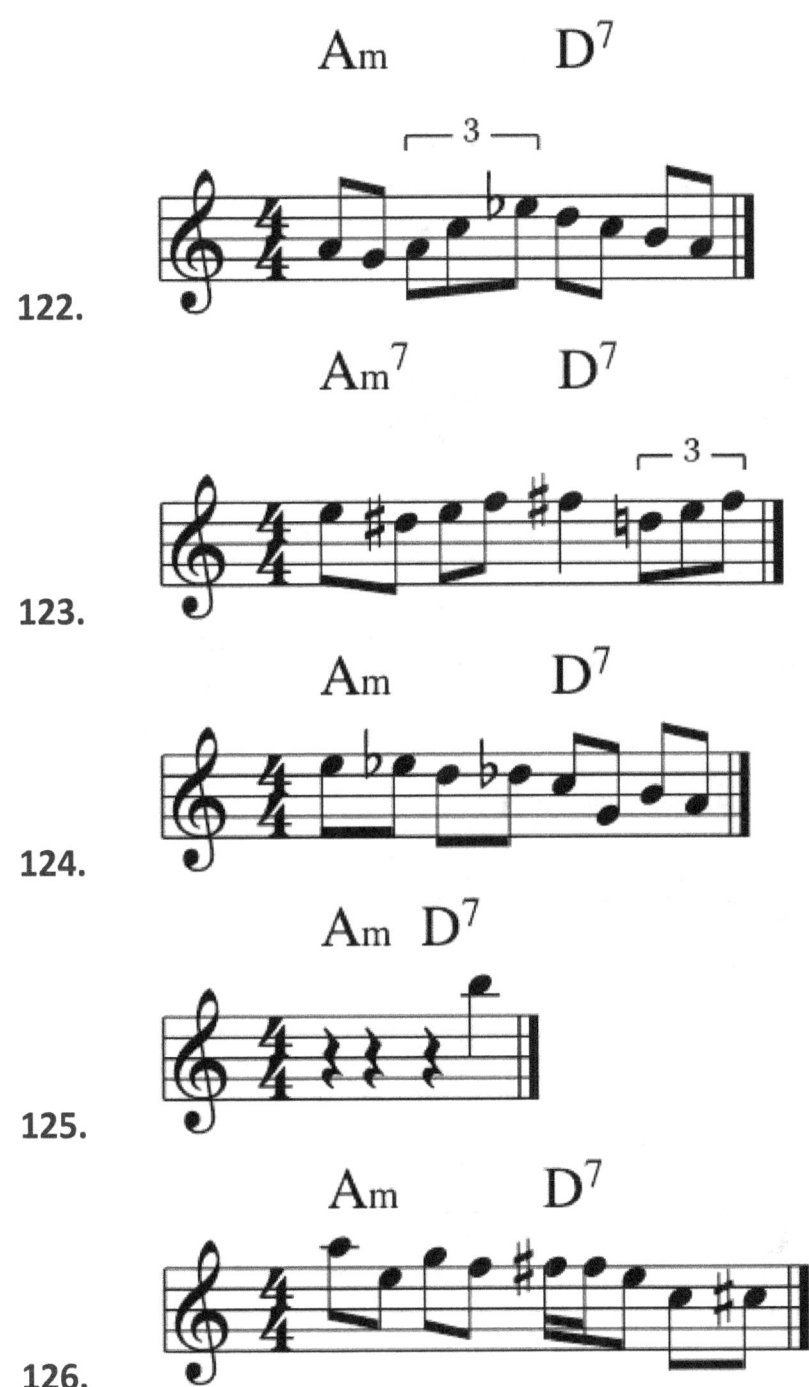

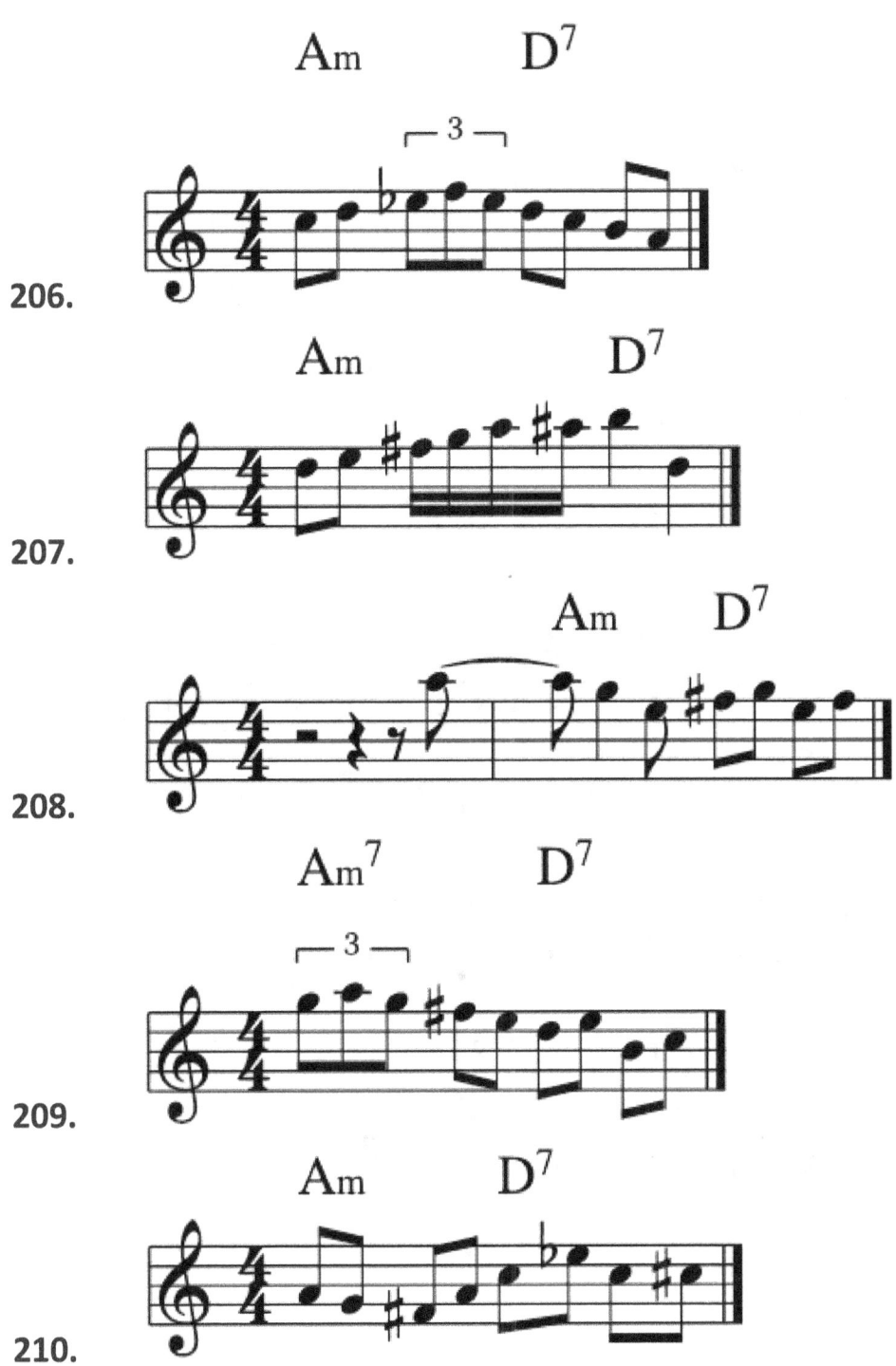

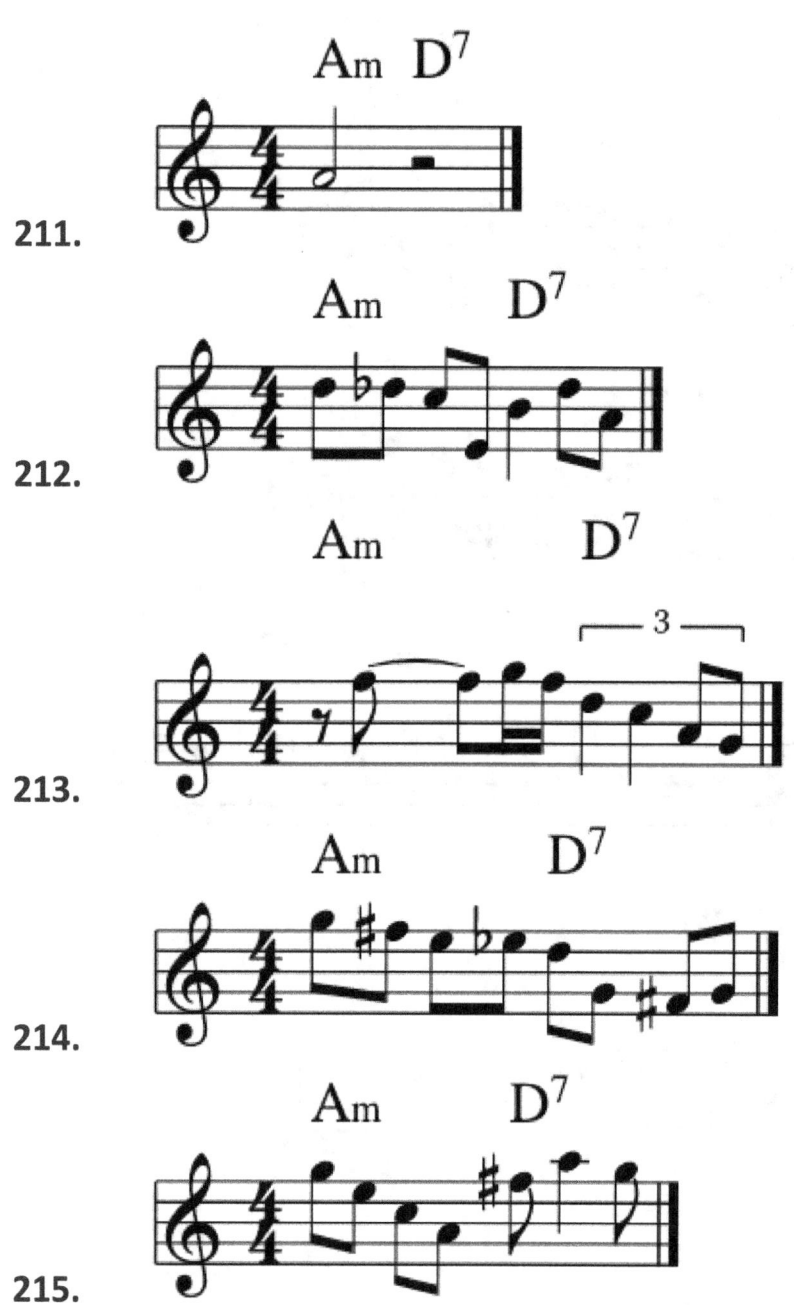

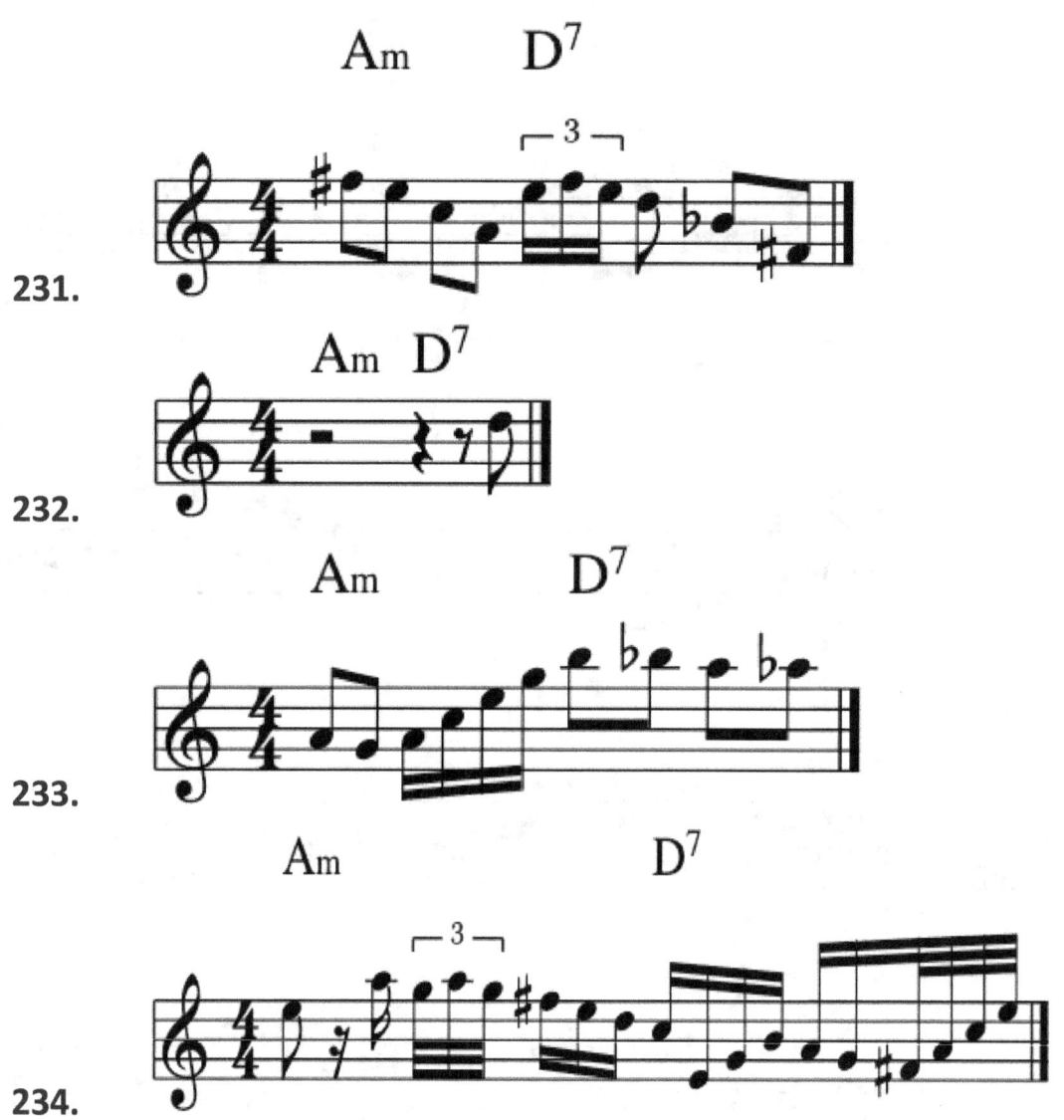

A min to E7

1.

2.

B min to B7

1.

B min to E7

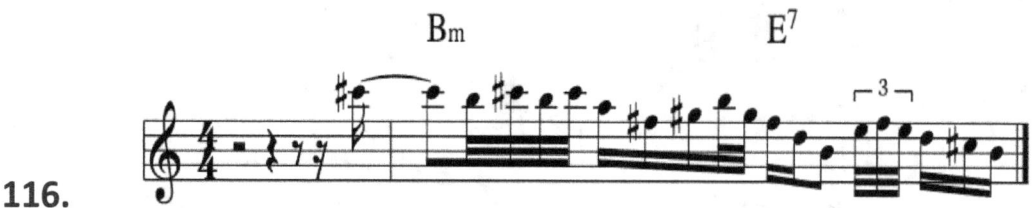

B min to F#7

C min to B7

C min to F7

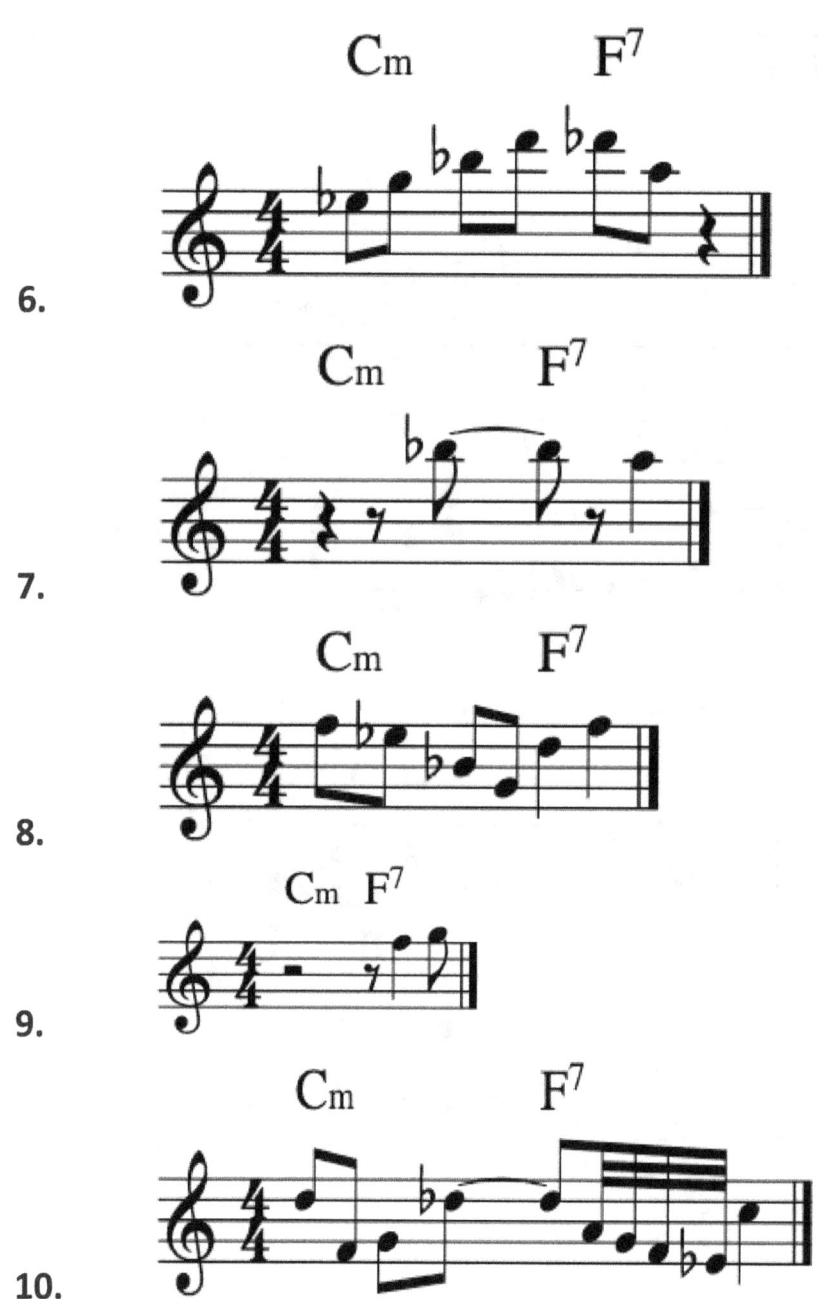

C# min to F#7

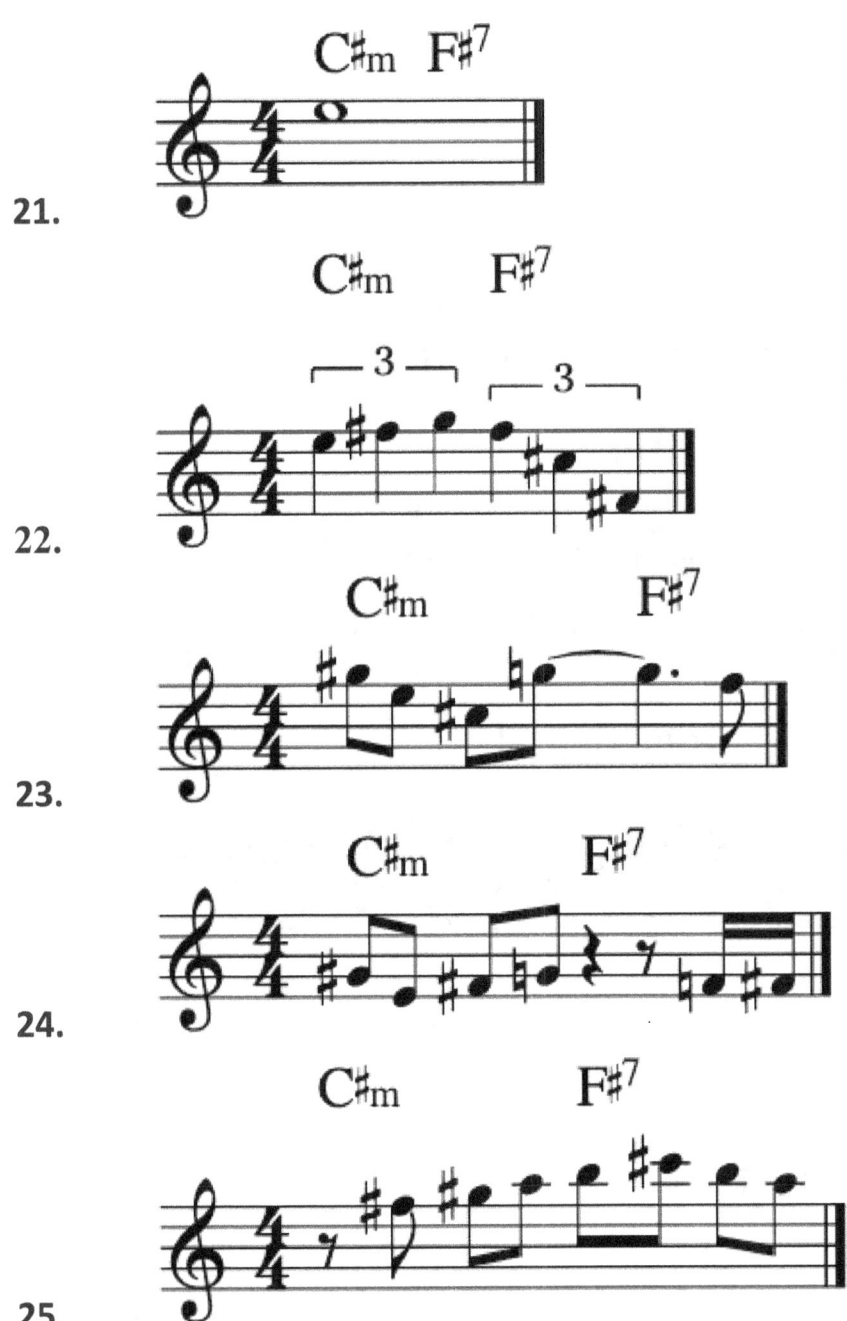

D min to Db7

D min to G7

79.

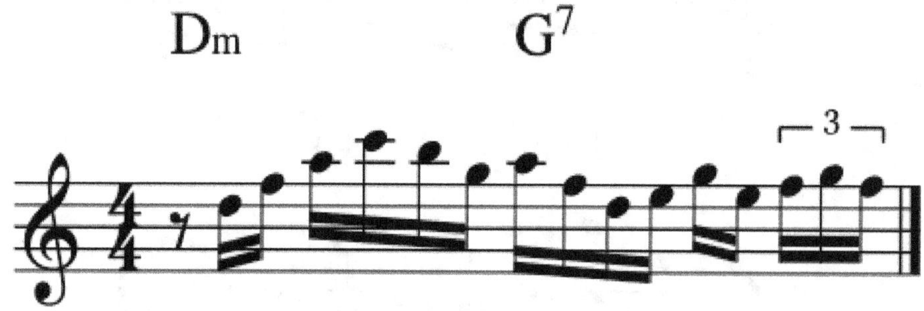

80.

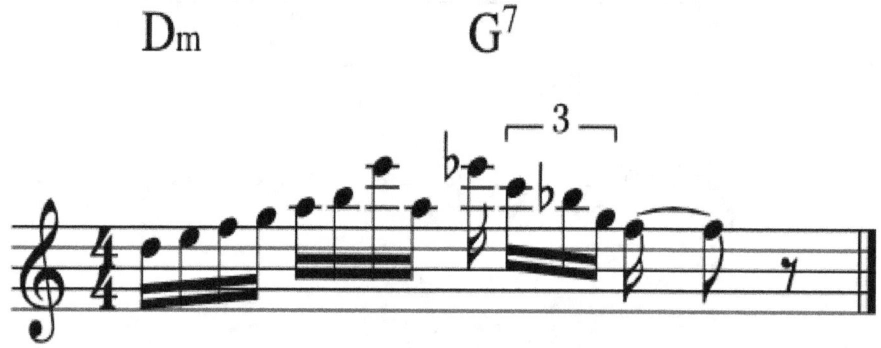

81.

E min to A7

1.

98.

99.

F min to Bb7

1.

2.

3.

F# min to B7

1.

2.

3.

14.

15.

16.

17.

G min to C7

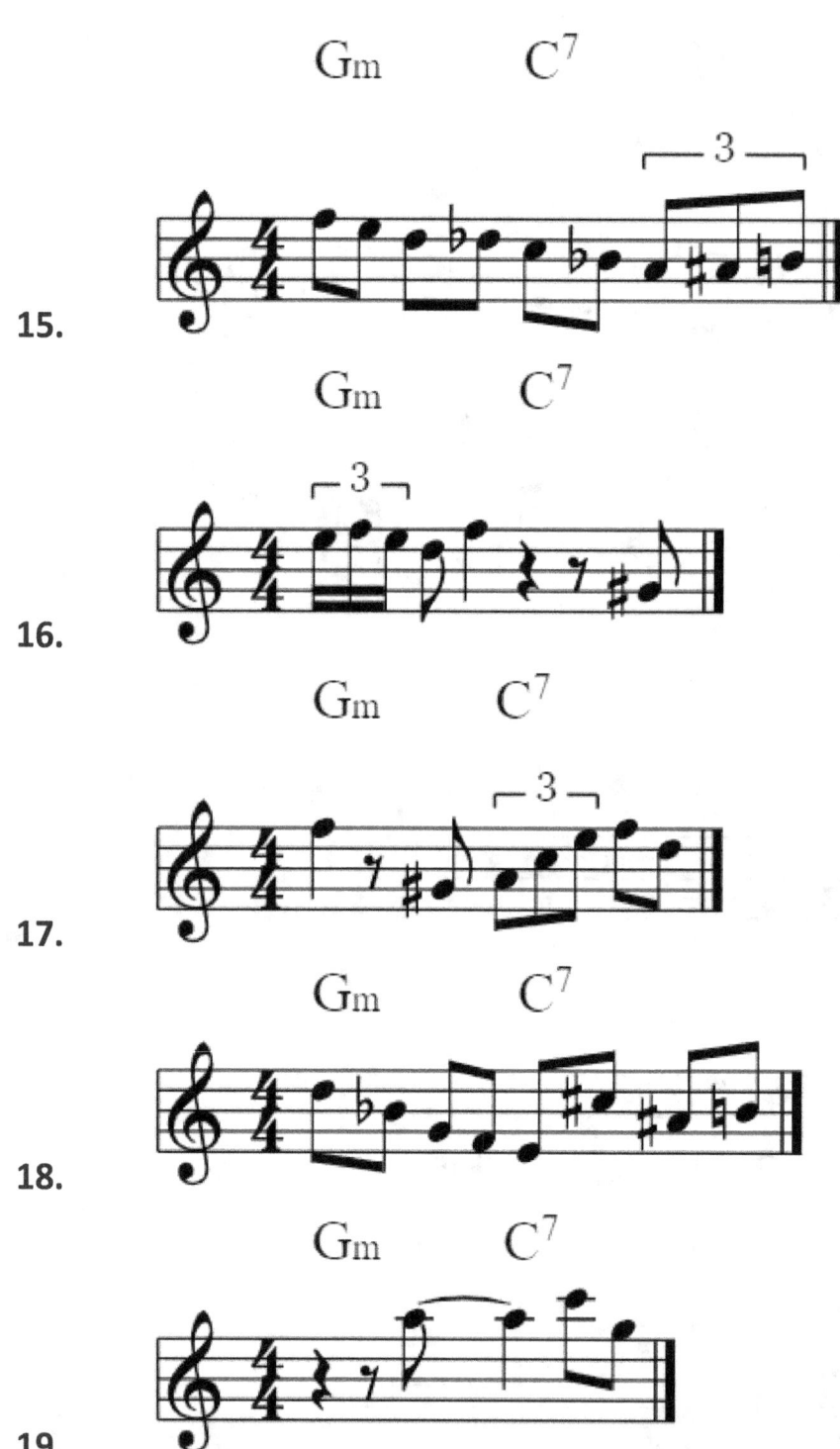

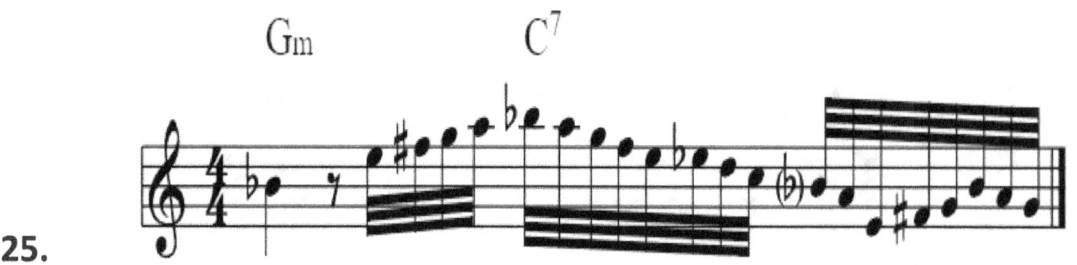

25.

G# min to C#7

1.

2.

Minor to Dominant 7b9:

A min to D7b9

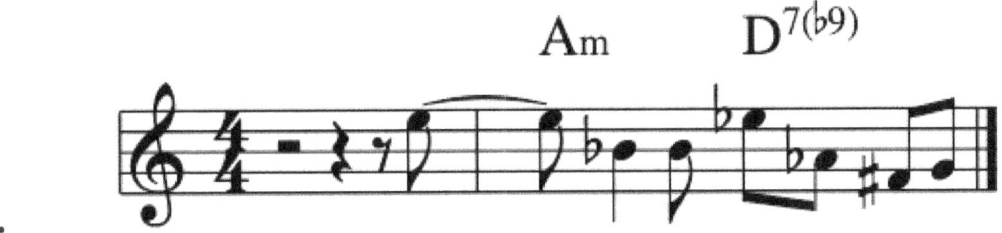

1.

B min to E7b9

1.

C# min to F#7b9

1.

2.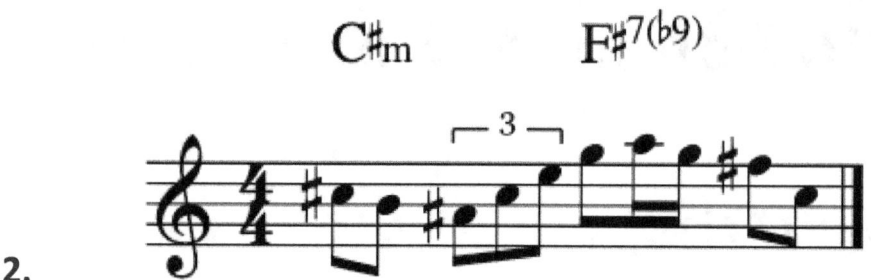

F# min to B7b9

1.

Minor to Dominant 7+9:

A min to D7+9

1.

B min to F#7+9

1.

E min to B7+9

1.

Minor to Minor:

A min to Ab min

1.

B min to Bb min

1.

2.

3.

D min to Db min

F# min to F min

Minor to Augmented 7:

A min to D7#5

2.

D min to G7#5

1.

E min to A7#5

1.

Minor to Dominant 7 to Dominant 7+9:

E min to A7 to A7+9

1.

Chapter #4

Half Diminished 7 ⦰ (Minor 7 b5) Chords and Progressions:

Half Diminished 7 ⦰ Chords:

E⦰7

1.

2.

Half Diminished 7 ⌀ Progressions:

Half Diminished 7 to Dominant 7:

A⌀7 to D7

1.

B⌀7 to E7

1.

2.

C#ø7 to F#7

D#ø7 to G#7

E ⌀7 to A7

F#⌀7 to B7

3.

4.

Half Diminished 7 to Dominant 7b9:

B ø7 to E7b9

1.

Half Diminished 7 to Dominant 7+9:
D#ø to G#7+9

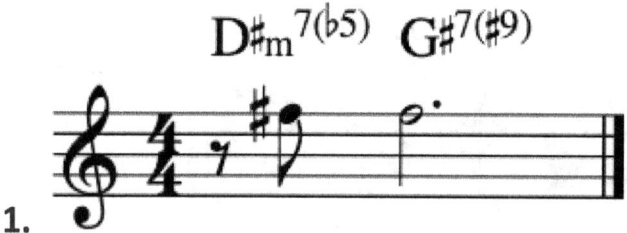

1.

Chapter #5

Fully Diminished Chords

Fully Diminished Chords:

C 0 (Fully Diminished)

1.

2.

3.

4.

D 0 (Fully Diminished)

1.

2.

3.

4.

G# 0 (Fully Diminished)

1.

2.

Chapter #6

Augmented Chords

Augmented Chords:

D+

1.

Augmented 7:

A+7

1.

2.

C+7

1.

D+7

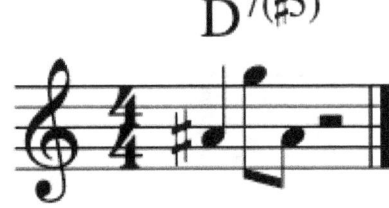

1.

2.

3.

G+7

REFERENCES

Ainsworth, J. (1970). Research project in creativity in music education. *Council for Research in Music Education, 22,* 43-48.

Aebersold, J., et al. (1978). *Charlie Parker Omnibook.* Hal Leonard Corporation.

Anderson, R. C, & Pichert, J.W. (1978). Recall of previously unrecallable information following a shift in perspective. *Journal of Verbal Learning and Verbal Behavior, 17,* 1-12.

Azzara, C. D. (1993). Audiation-based improvisation techniques and elementary instrumental students' music achievement. *Dissertation Abstracts International,* 53 (04), 1088A, (UMI No. 9223853).

Azzara, C. D., Grunow, R.F., & Gordon, E.E. (1997a). *Creativity in improvisation, Book 1.* Chicago: GIA.

Azzara, C. D., Grunow, R.F., & Gordon, E.E. (1997b). *Creativity in improvisation: Getting started.* Chicago: GIA.

Azzara, C. D., & Grunow, R.F. (2006). *Developing musicianship through improvisation.* Chicago: GIA.

Bartlett, F. (1958). *Thinking: An experimental and social study.* New York: Basic Books.

Bink, M. L., & Marsh, R. L. (2000). Cognitive regularities in creative activity. *Review of General Psychology, 4,* 59-78.

Boyle, J. D., & Radocy, R. E. (1987). *Measurement and evaluation of musical experiences.* New York: Schirmer Books.

Bransford, J. D., & Johnson, M. K. (1972). Contextual prerequisites for understanding: Some investigations of comprehension and recall. *Journal of Verbal Learning and Verbal Behavior, 11,* 717-726.

Bransford, J. D., & Johnson, M. K. (1973). Considerations of some problems of comprehension. In W.G. Chase (Ed.), *Visual information processing (pp.* 383- 438). New York: Academic Press.

Bruner, J. S. (1960). *The process of education.* New York: Vintage Books.

Bruner, J. S. (1966). *Toward a theory of instruction.* Cambridge: Harvard University Press.
Campbell, D. T., & Stanley, J. C. (1966). *Experimental and quasi-experimental designs for research.* Chicago, IL: Rand-McNally.

Carlson, W. R. (1980). A procedure for teaching jazz improvisation based on an analysis of the performance practice of three major jazz trumpet players: Louis Armstrong, Dizzy Gillespie, and Miles Davis. *Dissertation Abstracts International,* 42(03), 1042A, (UMINo. 8118663).

Colwell, R. (1970). *Music achievement tests.* Chicago: Follett Educational Corporation.

Consortium of National Arts Education Association. (1994). *National standards for arts education: What every young American should know and be able to do in the arts.* Reston, VA: Music Educators National Conference.

Delia Pietra, C. J., & Campbell, P. S. (1995). An ethnography of improvisation training in a music methods course. *Journal of Research in Music Education,* 43(2), 112- 126.

DiBlasio, D. (2011). *Pathways to Improvisation: A Reference for Teaching and Learning to be a Great Improvisor.* Northeastern Music Publications.

Douglas, K. (2006). The effects of a music learning theory-based pattern instruction improvisation curriculum on the improvisational ability of secondary instrumental music students. *Dissertation Abstracts International,* 44(04), 1584A (UMI
No. 1432177).

Finke, R., Ward, T., & Smith, S. (1992). *Creative cognition: Theory, research, and applications.* Cambridge, MA: MIT Press.

Flohr, J. (1979). Musical improvisation behavior of young children. *Dissertation Abstracts International. 40(10),* 5355A, (UMINo. 8009033).

Flohr, J. (1985). Young children's improvisations: emerging creative thought. *Creative Child and Adult Quarterly, 10,* 79-85.

Gagne, R. M. (1965). *The conditions of learning.* New York: Holt, Rinehart & Winston. Gagne, R. M. (1985). *The conditions of learning* (4th ed.). New York: Holt, Rinehart &

Gordon, E. E. (1965). *Musical aptitude profile, Manual.* Boston, Houghton Mifflin.

Gordon, E. E. (1971). *The psychology of music teaching.* Englewood Cliffs, NJ: Prentice-Hall.

Gordon, E. E. (1979). *Primary measures of music audiation.* Chicago: GIA.

Gordon, E. E. (1997a). *Learning sequences in music: Skill, content, and patterns* (5th ed.). Chicago: GIA.

Gordon, E. E. (1997b). *Study guide for learning sequences in music.* Chicago: GIA.

Gordon, E. E. (1998a). *Harmonic improvisation readiness record and rhythm improvisation readiness record, Manual.* Chicago: GIA.

Gordon, E. E. (1998b). *Harmonic improvisation readiness record.* Chicago: GIA.

Gordon, E. E. (1998c). *Rhythm improvisation readiness record.* Chicago: GIA.

Gordon, E. E. (2003). *Learning sequences in music: Skill, content, and patterns* (6th ed.). Chicago: GIA.

Gordon, E. E. (2007). *Learning sequences in music: A contemporary music learning theory.* Chicago: GIA.

Guilbault, D. M. (2004). The effect of harmonic accompaniment on the tonal achievement and tonal improvisations of children in kindergarten and first grade. *Journal of Research in Music Education, 52 (1),* 64-76.

Guilford, J. P. (1956). The structure of intellect. *Psychological Bulletin, 53,* 267-293. Guilford, J. P. (1959). Traits of Creativity. In H.H. Anderson, (Ed.), *Creativity and its Cultivation,* (pp. 142-161). New York: Harper & Row

Karas, J. (2006). The effect of aural and improvisatory instruction on fifth grade band students' sight-reading ability. *Dissertation Abstracts International,* 66(12), 4334A, (UMI No. 3199697).

Koestler, A. H. (1964). *The act of creation.* New York: Macmillan.

Kratus, J. (1991). Growing with improvisation. *Music Educator's Journal, 78(4),* 26-29.

Madsen, C. K. (Ed.). (2000). Housewright declaration. In *Vision 2020: The housewright symposium on the future of music education,* (pp. 219-220). Reston, VA: Music Educators National Conference.

Marsh, R. L., Landau, J. D., & Hicks, J. L. (1996). How examples may (and may not) constrain creativity. *Memory & Cognition, 24,* 669-680.

Marshall, H. D. (2002). Effect of song presentation method on pitch accuracy of third grade children. *Dissertation Abstracts International,* 64(01), 91 A, (UMI No. 3079131).

McPherson, G. (1993/94). Evaluating improvisational ability of high school instrumentalists. *Council for Research in Music Education, 119,* 11-20.

Montano, D. R. (1983). The effect of improvisation in given rhythms on rhythmic accuracy in sight reading achievement by college elementary group piano students. *Dissertation Abstracts International,* 44(06), 1720A, (UMI No. 8323620).

Partchey, K. C. (1973) The effects of feedback, models, and repetition on the ability to improvise melodies. *Dissertation Abstracts International,* 35(01), 240A, (UMI No. 7416058).

Reinhardt, D. (1990). Preschool children's use of rhythm in improvisation. *Contributions to Music Education, 17,* 7-19.

Rowlyk, W. T. (2008). Effects of improvisation instruction on nonimprovisation music achievement of seventh and eighth grade instrumental music students. (Doctoral dissertation). Available from ProQuest Dissertations and Theses database. (UMI No. 3300374)

Sarath, E. (1993). Improvisation for global musicianship. *Music Educators Journal, 80(2),* 23-26.

Schenkel, S. M. (1980). A guide to the development of jazz improvisation skills in the jazz idiom. *Dissertation Abstracts International,* 41(03), 847A, (UMI No. not available).

Schleuter, S. L. (1988). *A sound approach to teaching instrumentalists.* OH; Kent State University Press.

Schmidt, C. P., & Sinor, J. (1986). An investigation of the relationships among music audiation, musical creativity, and cognitive style. *Journal of Research in Music Education, 34,* 160-172.

Shadish, W. R., Cook, T. D., & Campbell, D. T. (2002). *Experimental and quasi- experimental designs for generalized causal inference.* New York: Houghton Mifflin.

Shamrock, M. (1990). Process and improvisation in Orff-Schulwerk. In P. Carder (Ed.), *The eclectic curriculum in American music education* (pp. 151-160). Reston, VA: Music Educators National Conference.

Smith, S. M., Ward, T. B., & Schumacher, J. S. (1993). Constraining effects of examples in a creative generation task. *Memory & Cognition,* 21, 837-845.

Swanwick, K. (1988). *Music, mind, and education.* London: Routledge.

Torrance, E. P. (1962). *Guiding creative talent.* Englewood Cliffs, NJ: Prentice-Hall. Torrance, E. P. (1963). *Education and the creative potential.* Minneapolis, MN: University of Minnesota Press.

Torrance, E. P. (1970). *Encouraging creativity in the classroom.* Dubuque, IA: Wm. C. Brown Co.

Torrance, E. P. (1972), Can we teach children to think creatively? *Journal of Creative Behavior, 6(2),* 114-143.

Torrance, E. P. (1974). *The Torrance tests of creative thinking: Norms-technical manual.* Bensenville, IL: Scholastic Testing Service.

Wallas, G. (1926). *The art of thought.* New York: Harcourt, Brace, & Company. Walters, D. L., & Taggart, C. C. (1989). *Readings in music learning theory.* Chicago: GIA.

Walters, D. L. (1992). Sequencing for efficient learning. In Cowell, R. (Ed.), *Handbook of research in music teaching and learning,* (pp. 535- 545). New York: Schirmer Books.

Yoder, M. D. (1996). *Beginning Jazz Improvisation*. Prentice-Hall.

Please enjoy our IOS APP-Pathways to Parker (Treble Clef)-

Ad Free PTP123TC

www.ingramcontent.com/pod-product-compliance
Lightning Source LLC
Chambersburg PA
CBHW080325020526
44117CB00036B/2804